WEIRD ONTARIO PLACES

Humorous, Bizarre, Peculiar & Strange Locations & Attractions across the Province

Dan de Figueiredo

BLUE
BIKE
BOOKS

D0067653

© 2006 by Blue Bike Books
First printed in 2006 10 9 8 7 6 5 4 3 2 1
Printed in Canada

All rights reserved. No part of this work covered by the copyrights hereon may be reproduced or used in any form or by any means—graphic, electronic or mechanical—without the prior written permission of the publisher, except for reviewers, who may quote brief passages. Any request for photocopying, recording, taping or storage on information retrieval systems of any part of this work shall be directed in writing to the publisher.

The Publisher: Blue Bike Books

Library and Archives Canada Cataloguing in Publication

De Figueiredo, Dan, 1964-
   Weird Ontario places : humorous, bizarre, peculiar and strange locations and attractions across the province / Dan de Figueiredo ; Roger Garcia, Graham Johnson, illustrators.

ISBN-13: 978-1-897278-07-9
ISBN-10: 1-897278-07-1

   1. Ontario—Miscellanea.   2. Ontario—Description and travel—Miscellanea. I. Title.

FC3061.6.D43 2006   971.3   C2006-903329-3

Project Director: Nicholle Carrière
Project Editor: Nicholle Carrière
Illustrations: Roger Garcia, Graham Johnson
Cover Image: Roger Garcia

We acknowledge the financial support of the Alberta Foundation for the Arts for our publishing program.

PC: P5

CONTENTS

DEDICATION

For Paul, who helped me rediscover my passion...
and then mocked me with it!

ACKNOWLEDGEMENTS

This book could not have been written without the generous help of a great many "weird" Ontarians and "weird" Canadians before them. First, I have to thank Blue Bike Books for letting me create the template for the series and asking me to contribute a second book to it! I also have to thank my editor, Nicholle Carrière, for wading through my original work and catching all the things that I wouldn't want most of you to see. I have again had a great time researching, writing and putting this provincial slice of weird together.

I also have to thank a great many people from the various government tourist offices, towns, sights and festivals. If I've forgotten anyone, I do apologize. But here is a list of people whose help was invaluable. They include:

Paul Figueiredo; Sharon Lindsay; Bob Lindsay; John Fisher; Bill Lishman; Jane Sims; Susan Ferrier Mackay; Lauren O'Malley; Ontario Tourism Marketing Partnership; Bev Carret, Manager, Government and Community Relations, Art Gallery of Ontario; Eunice Henning (the big Adirondack chairs); Marissa Harvey, Marketing and Communications Services Coordinator, Niagara Parks Commission; Sarah Wood, Events and Public Relations Manager, Niagara Parks Commission; Statistics Canada (2001 Community Profiles, released June 27, 2002); Jean-Pierre Ouellette, Clerk and Community Development Manager, Town of Cochrane; Fred Veale, Canada Curling Stone, London, Ontario; Reena Greer and Rebecca Ward, City of Toronto; Michael O'Connor, MJO Studios (Dorion murals); John Hildebrandt, Beth Hildebrandt, Morris Towns (Barry's Bay Avro Arrow); Liane Kotler, TV Ontario, *Studio 2*; Bob Bratina, Councillor, Ward 2, Hamilton; Henry Jongerdon, Royal Botanical Gardens; Simon, my dog and constant companion, who gets to hear the first draft of absolutely everything.

I thank all of the above for their directions, clarifications, redirections, fact-checking and all-around assistance with this, my second little weird book. I hope to run into some of you on my future travels.

INTRODUCTION

Weird Ontario Places is the follow-up to my book *Weird Canadian Places*. In that book, I looked into the weirdest places across the country. Now I get to include all the places (in Ontario) that didn't make it into the previous book, because I had to make room for the other provinces and territories. In this one, Ontario doesn't have to share!

And that's good, because Ontario is a large place. It's the largest province in the country in terms of population (11,410,046) and the second largest province in terms of area (916,733 km²)—only Québec is larger. Ontario is home to Canada's largest city, Toronto, at 2,481,494 people, and the nation's capital, Ottawa. It also contains places that are large, below us, above us, record-breaking, screaming, ghostly, ghoulish, freaky, foolish, monstrous, celebratin', alien, naturally wonderful, distinctive, memorable, marked and just plain weird.

I'm talking about places to visit and gawk at in awe such as the largest free-standing structure in the world (for the time being anyhow); those displaying the raw power of a waterfall or the ability to draw tourists and tackiness alike; or a large ark not built by Noah or my upstairs neighbour; and a very large sundial that may or may not be a folly.

These are the things that Ontarians' dreams are made of. And we're not afraid to sing it out loud. Do you remember the 1970s tourist ads for Ontario and their inspired jingle? It went something like this:

A place to stand,
A place to grow,
Ontari-ari-ari-ohhhh!

If that's not weird, wild and wonderful, I don't know what is. And here we come to my definition of "weird." To me, weird means odd, unique, interesting, out of the ordinary, not mundane and also fun! It can include the mystical, the paranormal and the unexplained. It encompasses things described as queer, incomprehensible and mysterious. It can be connected with fate, warning or just plain size. So you see, it's a word that can include a great many and varied things.

The question "why" is at the heart of "weird"—it defines the weirdness. Why is Toronto's Royal Bank Tower covered in 24-carat gold? Why does Exeter have white squirrels that aren't albino? Why does Father Goose live underground and build a replica of Stonehenge out of crushed cars?

Weird does not, in my mind, have a bad connotation, though I do accept that many people got weirded out when I called them and said I was writing a book on weird Ontario places and wanted to include their place.

My angle of attack in writing the book was to utilize humour, because I really don't take anything too seriously. Laughter is my universal filter and I have employed it here with glee and hopefully with success! You'll notice that my tongue is firmly planted in my cheek as I talk of each and every one of my weird finds. I wanted to play with all the weirdness that is Ontario as I did with Canada before it. My intention is not to offend, and I hope that everyone who reads this book will take my observations, questions, extrapolations and wit in the spirit with which I wrote them. I really hope that people will be entertained. If you learn a little something, that's okay, too.

My research has afforded me the opportunity to learn a great deal about this odd and sprawling province. There are now a great many places in Ontario that I want to visit, though a few months ago I did not think so. I am fascinated by the paranormal, intrigued by the oddities that nature has to offer and celebrate all that is kitschy. I'd love to see the ghost lights of Scugog, visit the Donnelly tombstone and enjoy a Pilsner in a stein in Kitchener. I have actually seen one UFO, and would love to see more. Perhaps go for a spin in a flying saucer or alien craft, if that's what they are. So, if there's a list somewhere, someone please put me on it. That's the weird that this book is about.

The choices I've made are somewhat arbitrary. My interpretation of what is interesting, odd and weird is probably different from what others would designate as weird. However, I'm the one who wrote the book, so enjoy it or go write your own. There are so many weird places that I don't think I've even covered half of them. I suspect that the number will just continue to grow. Who knows, maybe there'll be a *Weird Ontario Places, Volume 2.*

There may be a great many weird Ontario "things" that I have omitted. However, the parameters of this book were specific to weird "places." Some weird things crossed over and could be directly pegged to place. A great many of the weirdest "things" do not lend themselves to this type of specificity, so they got tossed. I also tended to avoid places considered weird just because of their place names. Those weird places that made it to final cut also tend to be current, ongoing and recurring sites of weirdness. In general, I avoided one-offs, lone occurrences and, except in a very few instances, weird places that are only weird because of some thing or things that happened in the past.

Peppered throughout the book you will read all about the various large things, record-breaking things and marks that make many places in Ontario very weird. The large ones next to a road, highway or path tend to be my favourites, because they've been lifted on high by some ambitious person or community that wants to take their little piece of heaven from relative obscurity to must-see tourist stop and don't mind achieving this goal by becoming a weird little oddity. Whether their claim to fame is the "World's Largest Snowman" or a world-famous fish, who cares! If you build it big, tourists will come a-runnin' with cameras in hand and flashes a-flashin'.

Remember—it's a place to stand, a place to grow, Ontari-ari-ari-ohhhh!

Dan de Figueiredo

What Lies Underneath

Often when we look up at things not always in plain sight or dig deep beneath the common, everyday, readily readable stuff, we discover a whole weird world of wonder, a spooky or surprising underbelly, or perhaps an overhang, a hanger-on or something that just won't be ignored!

What I'm talking about and what we'll look at in the next two chapters are the weirdest places you'd never be able to spot unless you knew they were there and the ones you can't possibly miss because they won't let you—the little hidden gems literally beneath the ground and others that are not only out in the open but scream "Look at me!" It's human-made monstrosity vs. little hidden wonder; odd urban architecture vs. Cold War bunker; weathervane vs. mall; 24-carat-gold glass vs. dirt mound; haunted tunnel vs. underground igloo—you get the idea. Here are Ontario's underground wonders and aboveground screamers.

THE DIEFENBUNKER
CARP

The promotional literature asks this question: "Looking for a different site for your tours to visit?" Well, you've definitely found it here. The Diefenbunker, as it is affectionately called, is one of those Cold War relics you'd think could only be found in the United States or Russia. But no, the Diefenbunker is real and is located just 35 kilometres east of Ottawa in the community of Carp...or should I more accurately say, underneath the community of Carp.

The Diefenbunker was built between 1959 and 1961 and was intended to house essential government and military personnel in case of a nuclear attack. It's a four-storey facility that was built into a hill and designed to survive a five-megaton blast a kilometre and a half away. Although the idea of such a Cold War relic serving as a Cold War museum is kitschy to say the least, the Historic Sites and Monuments Board of Canada has called the Diefenbunker "the most important surviving Cold War site in Canada." And it almost didn't survive.

When Canadian Forces Station Carp (the official name of the Diefenbunker) was closed in 1994, the government gutted the facility. Some of its original artifacts were dispersed to the Canadian War Museum, the Canadian Museum of Civilization and the Military Communications and Electronics Museum in Kingston, but most of the stuff disappeared for good. However, the museum's staff has done an amazing job of begging, borrowing and stealing (not literally) original artifacts and recreating others to fill the Diefenbunker and give it a real sense of its Cold War–era prime.

A 90-minute tour of the meandering facility takes visitors through a time warp to the 1960s. You get to experience the blast tunnel, the airlock, the top-level hallway, the Federal Warning Centre, the machine room, the CBC Radio studio, the Bank of Canada vault, the War Cabinet room and the prime minister's suite and offices.

And I'll bet that in the cramped prime minister's quarters you can well imagine Prime Minister John Diefenbaker, with his jowls a-flappin', practising his less-than-stellar French while commanding Canada's response to a nuclear attack—which I believe was officially sitting and waiting to see what the Americans would do. For a weird and wacky blast from the past, the Diefenbunker is high on my list of special places.

And here's something else to consider—since the Diefenbunker was abandoned in 1994, where does Canada's governing elite plan to take refuge in case something "bad" happens? Have they just abandoned the idea of bunkers altogether, putting themselves on the same level as the hoi polloi? Think about our prime ministerial types; Brian Mulroney, Jean Chrétien, Paul Martin and Stephen Harper would want to save their skins for our sakes, of course, if some nuclear fallout or terrorist-inspired incident were to happen, don't you think? So, just where do they plan to run...I mean, hide out...I mean, shelter themselves for the good of us all? Perhaps there is something more to the prime minister's retreat at Harrington Lake than we've officially been told? There's got to be at least more than one bathroom, anyway. Perhaps there's even a ferret hole entrance to a giant safe room and/or bunker facility? I don't know for sure, but I'd guess there is a new, more modern version of the Diefenbunker somewhere near the National Capital Region. If anyone knows about it, drop me a line. I can keep a secret. No, really!

Bigfoot

It's a Bigfoot, it's an ape, it's my Uncle Mel in a diaper, smoking a cigar? Well, the pictures of this roadside Sasquatch in Vermilion Bay (west of Dryden) could be any of the above. I've got no idea who the artist was and I'm betting he wants to keep it that way. The—for the sake of argument, we'll call it "Bigfoot"—Bigfoot is 5.5 metres tall and sits near the Trans-Canada Highway in front of a gas station. And he looks angry, my friends! His arms are outstretched and his thumbs reach into the sky. That's why some people think he's hitchhiking. Or perhaps he's just mocking the Fonz or Lindy Englund? I personally think his hands form a rude gesture, but he's a Bigfoot and has gotten the fingers mixed up. There is apparently a speaker inside the statue, which allows the gas station's owners to mess with people's heads by having Bigfoot talk to them. I hear a couple from Ohio talked back. No, really!

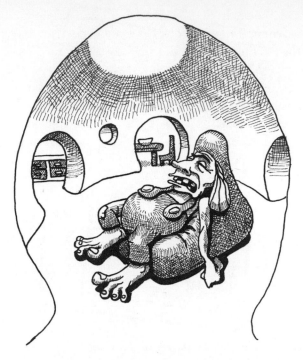

THE LISHMAN HOUSE
BLACKSTOCK

How does a home that was featured in magazines such as *Harrowsmith* and *Canadian Architect* as well as on the CBC-TV show *Life and Times* qualify as underground and weird? Well, the "hole" thing has to do with its designer, builder and occupant, Bill Lishman. You could even say that this home transformed its designer from igloo enthusiast to mole man.

That's because Bill Lishman's home is a series of eight interconnected, igloo-like domes that were built with wire-mesh frames, covered with concrete and a bunch of waterproofing materials and then covered over with dirt. An igloo was actually Lishman's original inspiration for the structure.

The home features in-floor heating, overhead skylights and a roof that requires mowing. The whole unique structure reminds one of the dwelling where Luke Skywalker grew up. You know, the one owned by Uncle Owen and Aunt Beru. There isn't a right angle to be seen. The arched doorways are handmade, as is the furniture inside the home—even the refrigerator is round. It pops out of the kitchen counter at the touch of a button just like in the 1996 film *Fly Away Home*. Which is no great surprise, since that film, about a man who taught geese to fly behind an ultralight plane, is based on the life of our home's designer, Bill Lishman.

KAY-NAH-CHI-WAH-NUNG (MANITOU MOUNDS)
STRATTON

Kay-Nah-Chi-Wah-Nung ("Place of the Long Rapids"), near Rainy River, is the sight of some of the most interesting underground archaeological sites in the country. As the press information says: "Kay-Nah-Chi-Wah-Nung and the surrounding lands hold the record of almost 8000 years. The Place of the Long Rapids contains the largest group of burial mounds and associated village sites in Canada."

And just what are these mounds and why are they so significant? The mounds are essentially a burial place used originally by the Laurel culture (300 BC–1100 AD). The Laurel are thought to be the first group of First Nations people to have built mounds at this site, but not the only ones. The Laurel mounds are up to 7 metres in height and 18 to 24 metres in diameter. The mound builders would dig a shallow pit, place the deceased inside and cover the remains with earth. Over hundreds of years, more deceased were placed on top and covered with earth. The layering process created the mounds as they are seen today. Sometimes the dead were buried with items that they used in life that their people thought they would also need in death. Things such as medicine bags, pipes, food, clay pots and tools have been uncovered.

The Manitou Mounds site includes a visitor centre that explores the site as a ceremonial centre, its context within North America and the culture of the Ojibwa peoples. It's a fascinating look back into the past of First Nations people and their burial rituals.

THE PHANTOM SUBWAY STATION
TORONTO

Myth, folklore, urban legend or reality—that's what people have been asking for decades about the notorious phantom subway station known as Lower Bay. Well, I am happy to tell all that the phantom station does, in fact, exist. This will come as no surprise to older folks who were around when the station was

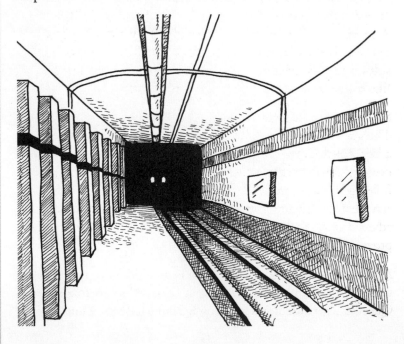

actually used way back in 1966. So how was it used, why isn't used anymore, and how has the myth surrounding it grown? Hold your horses—I'm getting to it!

So as not to bore those who don't give a flip about Toronto's subway, I'll keep it short. Basically, when the Bloor–Danforth line opened in 1966, Lower Bay was a transfer point between the University line (Lower Bay) and the Bloor–Danforth line (Upper Bay) in a similar way that the two lines still cross at St. George.

Lower Bay was also connected by a second tunnel to Museum Station, just like the one that connects Museum and St. George on the Spadina line. The three stations formed a "Y" configuration, with the idea that every second train heading north on the University line could take the right "Y" leg through Lower Bay and then would connect to the Bloor–Danforth line before it got to Bloor Station.

The system actually ran this way for six months, but the configuration was abandoned because it was confusing for passengers (and I suspect for readers who have never been on the TTC). Also, this "Y" configuration meant that the whole subway system was interconnected, so a single problem anywhere on either subway line disabled the entire system instead of just one line, like it does now.

So Lower Bay became all but abandoned, and the myth grew. The station is still accessible from Upper Bay by those who have a key. Much of the time, it is used by film companies to shoot creepy subway scenes, which is probably where the myth about it being haunted arose. There are also stories of people who have travelled the "phantom tunnel" to get to Lower Bay, but it is not advised, since the route is very dangerous and exploring it could prove fatal.

A second "phantom station," which is more like a roughed-in underground streetcar stop, exists at Lower Queen (Yonge and Queen). There are, however, no official documents about a third phantom station at Lower Osgoode. Official word from the TTC is that it doesn't exist. There are still whispers, though. Perhaps that's where the new Diefenbunker is located?

THE SCREAMING TUNNEL
NIAGARA REGION

This one falls under the heading of underground and creepily weird! The tunnel in question is not far from Queen Elizabeth Way on Warner Road near Garner Road. I've been there, and the tunnel is dark and smells of sulphur, not to mention that it's often full of water and empty beer bottles and used by younger folks for...oh, never mind.

It's either an abandoned or never-used railway tunnel that may have been built by the Grand Trunk Railway. The legend goes that if you light a match or lighter (any small flame will do) while you're standing in the centre of the tunnel, you'll hear a bone-chilling scream and your flame will blow out! Some variations on this legend say you have to light the match at midnight.

The explanation for the screaming and blowing out is something to do with an abused girl (now a ghost) who has a phobia of fire—that's why she screams and blows out the flames.

Some stories claim that the girl was set on fire by her father in an awful divorce dispute. Others claim she was raped in the tunnel (though that explanation doesn't link to the flame thing very well). Still others say the girl ran screaming and alight from a nearby burning farmhouse and died in the tunnel. The stories are as varied and creepy as you can imagine, which matches this dark and stinky tunnel toe to toe for its creep factor. Visit it in the light or the dark. Either way, it'll creep you out. Oh, and have fun!

JOURNEY BEHIND THE FALLS
NIAGARA FALLS

Niagara's "Journey Behind the Falls" is one of the weirdest of the weirdest of the weird. Weird, huh? When you get to the next-to-last chapter, the Weirdest of the Weird, this will make more sense. For now, enjoy the alliterative qualities of the above sentence and then read on.

Here's what I'm talking about: you take an elevator ride 38 metres down into the heart of the Niagara Escarpment. Once there, you are treated to a labyrinth of tunnels that meander behind the falls. Heading down one tunnel, there are viewing portals located directly behind the great falls. The force of the water is absolutely incredible. That behind-the-falls scene in *Last of the Mohicans* with Daniel Day Lewis is nothing compared to this!

Then you make your way back and head down the second tunnel, which takes you to an outside viewing platform far below the rim of the great gorge. And there it is—the awesome power of Niagara, right in front of you. The falls are to your right, and you can look up and see them crash 13 storeys into the gorge below. Out in front of you is the gorge and the powerful Niagara River slipping away to your left. The sound on this viewing platform is deafening, the sight is awe-inspiring and the absolute drenching wetness of the water is, well, drenching—even with the free, cookie-cutter, non-stylish, yellow rain poncho they provide for visitors. You're going to get wet no matter what!

Now, the weirdest thing about this is that everything I've described is real. It's not a simulator ride or a movie or animation. It's the power of Niagara right there in front of you. And it's completely safe—or so they say! Definitely a weird place!

BIG
GARGANTUAN &
RIDICULOUSLY
OVERSIZED

Chimo

The town of Cochrane has a population of 5690 people and one fibreglass polar bear named "Chimo." Chimo is a First Nations word meaning "friendly" and that's probably a good thing to be if you're a polar bear that greets people as they enter the town where the Polar Bear Express originates. That's right, Cochrane is the southern terminus of that venerable train that travels from Cochrane to "the edge of the Arctic" at Moosonee—a 300-kilometre journey that takes four and a half hours. Despite its beautiful scenery and spectacular service, there is controversy here. It seems Chimo wasn't good enough to be the official mascot of the Polar Bear Express. No sirree, Bob! Ontario Northland went and hired another polar bear and came up with the brilliant name "Choo Choo Bear." ☞

BIG GARGANTUAN & RIDICULOUSLY **OVERSIZED** In this bear-pit of controversy, I fall firmly on Chimo's side. I mean, Choo Choo Bear? Come on! It sounds like it was named by government bureaucrats to fulfill a particular politically correct niche, doesn't it? Ontario Northland claims the name was chosen by school children. If that's true, the children's bureaucrat parents probably prompted them. Anyway, Choo Choo Bear rides the rails in summer and performs mascot duties at festivals, fairs, schools and other functions during the rest of the year. Chimo—my buddy—doesn't need to perform here, there and everywhere. He stands tall, proud and stoi-cally in his place at the entrance to Cochrane. Besides, Chimo is 10.7 metres high and 10.7 metres long, whereas Choo Choo Bear is only the size of a man...because he's actually a guy dressed up in a Choo Choo Bear suit! Don't tell anyone, though. Some bureaucrats somewhere still think Choo Choo Bear is real.

Look Up,
Look Way Up

"Look up, look waaaaay up" is, of course, what the Friendly Giant used to say. For those of you not of my generation or who didn't watch TV as a kid, the Friendly Giant was a 15-minute-long children's show produced for many years by the Mother Corpse (CBC-TV), in which a giant of a man dressed in medieval garb (Bob Homme) interacted with a giraffe with blue spots and a chicken that was stuffed into a sack. The chicken's name was Rusty and the giraffe was called Jerome. The trio chatted—a lot— and also jammed together. Friendly played the recorder, Rusty was on harp and the giraffe? The giraffe sang—and what a voice! And what a weird little show.

Which brings me back to the weird places in this chapter. You see, everything in here seems to have taken on the Friendly Giant's saying: "Look up, look waaaaay up," with the additional "Oh come on, look at me. I'm really neato. They spent a lot of money on me, ya know!" Oh, and if you're looking up, don't forget to also look forward. I wouldn't want you to bump into anything and hurt yourselves...

ONTARIO COLLEGE OF ART AND DESIGN
TORONTO

The "Tabletop" at the Ontario College of Art and Design is one of the strangest additions to any building in a city quickly becoming known for strange additions to buildings. Designed by British architect Will Alsop, the Sharp Centre for Design, as it is officially known, looks as though a child's black-and-white checkerboard pencil box has been precariously balanced atop 12 multicoloured pencils. And yet it's all just an illusion—a little magic mixed with some architectural wonder. The black and white box is actually a very conventional two-storey structure that provides classroom and studio space and is held up by the elevator's central core (for those of you who care about engineering).

The Tabletop rests 26 metres in the air and allows great views of Toronto's downtown and Grange Park, which it backs onto along with the Art Gallery of Ontario. From dusk until midnight, 16 blue metal-halide lights illuminate the Tabletop, giving it a totally different look from its daytime configuration—sort of a purplish blue hue of a view!

Unfortunately, there are no public tours of the Sharp Centre, so you'll have to sneak your way inside or apply to become a student, I guess. However, the Tabletop is best viewed from the street, where one can't help but be enthralled by its charm. Kitschy, bright, odd, unique and wonderful, the Sharp Centre is everything an addition to a college of art should be! Outstanding or a stand out? Take your pick. However you look at it, this is one weird building that definitely screams "Look at me!"

BIG GARGANTUAN & RIDICULOUSLY OVERSIZED

Moonbeam

The municipality of Moonbeam, near Kapuskasing, has a flying saucer as a town landmark. Get it? Moonbeam...flying saucer? Located in Moonbeam's major town of New Liskeard, the flying saucer doesn't actually fly—it's anchored to the ground. So it's really more of an anchored saucer, I guess. It's 5.5 metres in diameter, 2.7 metres tall and has rotating flashing lights on its edges to replicate what Moonbeamian's think the real ones look like. I wonder if Steven Spielberg was consulted on the special effects, or doesn't he do that anymore because he's a serious film-maker now?

THE ART GALLERY OF ONTARIO (AGO)
TORONTO

Weird is something people have come to expect from world-renowned architect Frank Gehry—and his offering to the city in which he was born, while not quite as weird and wild as the undulating titanium structure in Bilbao, Spain, is nevertheless odd! It has all the hallmarks of becoming as inspirationally famous as Bilbao and has garnered praise, been heavily criticized and caused both glee and out-and-out disdain!

The promotional material screams: "Transformation AGO is the vision of a new kind of art museum." One with eyelashes, a sneeze guard or a fallen eyebrow, I would suggest. What am I talking about? Well, the entire north façade rises 21 metres above street level and is 183 metres long. There are two cuts, one each at the east and west extremities of the façade, which makes the building look as if it has two eyelashes that are raised on high and about to flutter shut. The PR person at the AGO compares them more to wings. Ohhhhhhhh!

Nevertheless, the centre portion of the front façade includes a 137-metre-long promenade on the second floor that allows visitors to look out onto traffic and streetcars on heavily congested Dundas Street, or affords those in their cars or on the streetcar a view inside the AGO while stuck in gridlock. This truly is an example of a museum giving back. And when you look at that centre structure of glass and Douglas-fir, you can't help but think salad bar sneeze guard. When you put the whole façade together and in context, it looks a lot like a Picasso-esque version of a fallen eyebrow...or so I think. I also think it is truly odd, wackily weird and positively wonderful, but come and see it for yourself when it is all complete in the spring of 2008.

ROYAL ONTARIO MUSEUM (ROM)
TORONTO

New and weird Toronto building number three is, I regret to say, my least favourite—though I suspect its designer could care less what I think. The building addition is definitely monumental, definitely costly and definitely big—it's also overhead and weird. But it looks way too much like it was ill-conceived and hastily constructed by Homer Simpson, and when it didn't work out, he beat it, bashed it and perhaps kicked it and then crammed it onto the Bloor Street side of the ROM, where maybe people wouldn't notice. "D-oh!" Does that sound harsh?

Let me start again. Since 1914, the Royal Ontario Museum has been thrilling adults and school groups alike with its dinosaurs, its exhibits of natural and cultural history and its really big totem pole (for those of us in Ontario, it's really big).

The ROM buildings themselves were from the beginning an amalgamation of various architectural influences. So, when it was announced that Daniel Libeskind's crystal-inspired design was going to be added to the north side, it was no great surprise. However, Libeskind's original design involved a lot of glass and a lot of light. The revised design involves a lot less glass, a lot less light and a whole bunch of metal cladding that screams "suburban backyard." This is not a criticism of suburban backyards—a corrugated metal shed fits there perfectly. I can't imagine a better place for it. But as an addition to one of the country's important cultural institutions, a shed seems, at best, out of place.

I have, of course, shortchanged the Libeskind shed-crystal design in one respect. It's not just a square, box-like shed. In fact, it's a bunch of boxes that have been piled on top of one another at different angles, so it appears more like a heap of old sheds awaiting the garbage man. Hmm, that's weird!

Oh, and don't just take my word for it, go to the ROM's own webcam (http://www.rom.on.ca/visit/webcam.php) and judge for yourself. Or plan a visit when the crystal-shed is finished and open to the public sometime in the fall of 2006.

BIG
GARGANTUAN &
RIDICULOUSLY
OVERSIZED

Homesteaders Museum

If you happen to be in northern Ontario and pass by Dymond, you must stop in at the Little Claybelt Homesteaders Museum, which will give you a fabulous taste of what life was like in Northern Ontario at the turn of the 20th century. And I'm thinking it was probably cold in winter and full of blackflies in summer! Anyway, if you don't have time for the museum, at least stop out front and have your picture taken with the statue of Ms. Claybelt. Ms. Claybelt is not a beauty queen in the traditional sense—oh, no! She is, in fact, a statu-esque replica, in an embellished and overgrown sense, of a Holstein cow. You see, the statue measures 3.7 metres by 5.5 metres, and anyone who's ever been near a real Holstein knows they never grow that big. Of course! But what a photo-op it is, anyway!

ROYAL BANK BUILDING
TORONTO

Are the bank towers in downtown Toronto really covered in gold? Well, when we're talking about Bay Street's twin Royal Bank towers, the answer is yes. The 14,000 windows of the two towers are coated with a thin layer of 24-carat gold. It apparently amounts to about 2500 ounces (71,000 grams) over the entire two buildings. So at the rate of $635 per ounce, which is the price of gold as I am writing this, the buildings' gold content alone is now worth about $1.6 million. And so, on sunny days or cloudy days or drizzly days or just about any day, the Royal Bank towers literally gleam, twinkle and sparkle with gold. And just why were the buildings built this way? Was it a way for the Royal Bank to stick it to customers and Canadians alike? Oh no, couldn't be! I mean, a bank wouldn't flaunt its opulence, would it? The official reason that the windows are covered in gold is that gold is a great insulator, so it reduces heating bills. No, really, that's what they'll tell you—with a straight face and without laughing! It's interesting that the buildings were constructed in 1976 and 1979, as Canada headed into a recession and people lost homes, businesses and livelihoods to banks building head offices of gold. But it was to keep their heating bills down. No, really! Just ask them.

ROBARTS LIBRARY, UNIVERSITY OF TORONTO
TORONTO

I like to call this one the "Turkey." It is, in fact, the third largest university library in North America, and I call it the Turkey not because it's an inferior building, nor because it makes gobbling noises, nor because I dislike it. I simply call it the Turkey because, as any idiot can see, from up close or from a distance, this grand research library resembles a large Thanksgiving bird. I'm currently looking at it out the window of my 22nd floor office near Yonge and Wellesley—and there it is, the Turkey, decked out in all its feathery finery.

The head of the turkey sticks up clearly at the intersection of Harbord and St. George Streets. If that tower with the beak on it was not meant to be a turkey's head, I can't say what the architect was thinking. The body consists of the big bulky, triangular-shaped main building with protruding concrete masses and glass that give it the look of plumage. And behind that, at the back of the building, there is a smaller annex section that looks like a tail.

Hey, don't take my word for it! Go see it for yourself. Critics, architects and students have decried this U of T landmark for its unfinished concrete face and its brutal, bunker-like style. But frankly, I think it's quite bold and forward-thinking of this institution of higher learning to plop the Turkey down right at its centre. Either that or the architect and the people who approved the building's construction are having a great laugh at the expense of the university and former premier John Robarts, for whom the building is named. Either way, the Turkey's worth a look...and perhaps a gobble, as well!

CANADA LIFE BUILDING
TORONTO

It's a beacon unto the city, perhaps even unto the world—
a weather beacon, that is. The flashing and cascading tower of
lights atop the wedding cake–like Canada Life Building have
had visitors and Torontonians mesmerized for more than a half
a century. Okay, maybe not mesmerized—I mean, it doesn't
stop traffic like the Gay Pride Parade or Caribana. But the
weather beacon on top of the Canada Life building at
330 University Avenue has, at the very least, intrigued people
more than just a little bit.

The beacon consists of two sets of lights: a cascading set of
lights on the sides of the tower and the box that rests on the

top. The lights on the sides of the tower cascade up when the temperature is rising, cascade down when the temperature is falling or are steady when the temperature is steady. The box at the top of the tower predicts approaching weather systems and is updated four times a day, seven days a week, thanks to Environment Canada. Red means cloudy skies, flashing white means snow, flashing red means rain, and green means skies are clear. The magical forecasting lights predict the weather during daylight hours and predict the next day's weather during the night.

So, for those of you visiting or living in old Hogtown, you're not paranoid. That building on University Avenue is really blinking at you, though not directly to you alone. And you can thank an insurance company for that reassurance...or should it be "re-insurance"? Either way, the beacon's got your back and has been a predictor of the near future, a light unto the city, since August 9, 1951. And they had a birthday party for it in 2001. Now that's weird!

CN TOWER
TORONTO

The CN Tower is one weird place, and not just because, at 553.33 metres in height, it is the world's tallest building. I mean, that does make it weird, but it's got a heightened weird factor because they've installed a glass floor, 342 metres above the ground. The see-through floor allows all but the faintest of heart to stand on the thick glass pane and look directly down at the ground. It makes you feel as though you are hovering in the air. That, my friends, is freakin' freaky! Go ahead and try it—you'll see! There is something oddly alarming about the feeling of looking straight down 342 metres. And for the sheer fear factor involved, the CN Tower has vaulted its way into the weird category.

The CN radio-TV-microwave tower, as I lovingly like to call it (because that's what it is), is weird in other ways. It has the highest public observation deck, the Skypod, at 447 metres above the ground. It also has a revolving restaurant 351 metres up called "360" because within 72 minutes one can sit, have dinner and see a 360-degree view of Toronto.

But I think possibly the weirdest thing about the CN Tower is the absolutely outrageous price of $26 plus tax that they charge each adult to go up this thing. I know kids get in for the bargain rate of $20 plus tax, but I think they've got some nerve charging this outrageous amount to take an elevator ride up into what the owners call "Canada's National Tower." Canada's National Tower, indeed! If it really was that, they'd charge five or six bucks for the thrill of this heightened weirdness—maybe seven for the glass floor. But $30 bucks for something that amounts to tall—I think not! The fact that people pay this extortion for "their" tower is the weirdest part of the whole thing. And that's my two cents—or 30 bucks if you use the CN Tower monetary conversion chart.

Where Fun Ghosts Roam with a Breath of Freak Air

Ghost stories have always scared the heck out of me. They still do. I started researching this chapter and the next late at night (that's 9:00 PM for me), but I had to stop almost as soon as I started, since I was getting really scared. I think I read the word "Boo" in the headline of a story and, well, it was lights out for me. Actually, it was book down and lights on for the rest of the evening. Even when I continued my research in the light of the next day, I got an uneasy feeling. Luckily, my dog Simon was there.

Not all ghosts are entirely scary. Some ghosts are even fun—they're relatively benign and not really into scaring, though flushing a toilet or two, cleaning ashtrays, whistling or mischievously borrowing things gives them a great thrill.

☞

This chapter deals with those kinds of fun-loving ghosts, as well as the ones that are good enough to stay in the great outdoors. The fresh-air freaks—ghosts, that is— include lost soldiers, lighthouse keepers, errant riders and sprites that like to light up cemeteries, as well as the canoe-paddling ghost of Tom Thompson. As a little treat (I hope) at the end of this chapter, I have reproduced my own personal ghost story. I have to admit, though, that it's not that scary. But then again, even ghosts as benign as Casper the Friendly Ghost really spook me!

So spend as much time as you want here reading about the fun-loving ghosts and their fresh-air freak counterparts— at least I know I will. As for the truly scary ghosts, look in the next chapter. Boy, I'm not looking forward to the next chapter... Actually, look in the next chapter to see if I actually had the nerve to go through with the next chapter.

WHERE THE FUN GHOSTS ROAM

MACKENZIE HOUSE
TORONTO

Does the rabble-rousing newspaper editor, the leader of the rebellions of 1837 and the first mayor of Toronto haunt this downtown Toronto house? Well, could be. There are, in fact, some people who think that Mackenzie House is the most haunted place in Toronto. There are also people who think that the statue of Winston Churchill at Nathan Phillips Square talks. I certainly don't think the latter is true. However, the haunting of Mackenzie House has a lot of supporters.

Mackenzie House is situated in the heart of downtown Toronto. It's a gaslit Greek Revival, Victorian rowhouse. Funny, how when you attach "Victorian" to something, it conjures up creepy nighttime images, including fog. Friends of W.L. Mackenzie took up a collection for him when he retired and bought the house. It changed hands several times after his death and was once even a boarding house. It's nearly been demolished a couple of times, but before the wreckers could start, something always saved it. Coincidence or ghostly happening? You be the judge.

The house has a fully functional 19th-century print shop like the one Mackenzie used to publish his rabble-rousing newspaper. It also apparently has a rabble-rousing ghost.

That's right! People claim to have seen the apparition of a short, bald man wearing a wig and a coat. Sounds like old William Lyon Mackenzie! Apparently old W.L.M. has a thing for the indoor plumbing. It wasn't there when he was an official "live" resident, but in his ghostly form, he likes to run the taps and set the toilet a-flushing. He was a rebel, remember—ahead of his time and an agent for change. So the restroom fascination seems completely in line.

There are a couple of other ghosts hanging out in the house as well—one may be the last Mrs. Mackenzie. If you want a first-hand glimpse, head down to 82 Bond Street in Toronto and just ask the staff about the ghosts and the exorcism. They'll be quite happy to tell you all about it. It's all an 1837-like rebellious hoot!

THE HERITAGE INN
CUMBERLAND

The Heritage Inn is located a short drive northeast of Ottawa in Cumberland. It's a distinctive three-storey stone building with a wraparound porch overlooking the Ottawa River. Over the years, it's been a home, a store, an inn, a doctor's office, a pharmacy and now serves as a restaurant. If you've been around for more than 100 years, I guess it's not unusual to have this many past incarnations. The inn is also said to be haunted, though the various reported happenings seem rather fun and benign. The spectre of a female ghost has often been seen walking through the inn's various dining areas. She won't take orders from guests, bus tables or even serve the food. However, the mystery woman, who is thought to have been a patient of the doctor who used to worked here, has a fun sense of humour and is duty bound. Items vanish on occasion, but more importantly, tables set themselves! I don't know about you, but if I worked there, I'd be glad for the help! The Heritage Inn is located at 2607 Montreal Road in Cumberland.

BIG
GARGANTUAN &
RIDICULOUSLY
OVERSIZED

Noah's Ark

You probably had no idea how roomy Noah's Ark actually was. I was certainly surprised to find out that in addition to the animals two by two, Noah had room for a pizza joint! I guess Noah was the world's first capitalist, and the Old Testament just glossed over that fact. So, what the heck am I talking about? Well, the good people who own and operate the family friendly resort and water park called Logos Land (that's an hour and half northwest of Ottawa, near Cobden) have built a replica of Noah's creaky old boat. Remember how the mean and spiteful Old Testament God told Noah to construct an Ark that measured 300 cubits long, 50 cubits wide and 30 cubits tall? Well, in the Logos Land version, God must have suggested some modifications that included a gift shop, large windows and a Pizza Hut. Now, before anyone goes accusing me of blasphemy, remember, I just report the oddities, I don't create them. And the oddest thing about this biblical replica with a capitalist twist is that there seems to be no place for animals in this Ark. Health department regulations, no doubt, have kept animal participation in the Logos Land Ark to the bits of ham and pepperoni that the "Hut" staff serve up on their pizzas. Praise the Lord and pass the Parmesan!

CHÂTEAU LAURIER
OTTAWA

The grande old girl of Ottawa, the Château Laurier, is a beautiful limestone castle built in the French Renaissance style. The general manager of the Grand Trunk Pacific Railway of Canada, Charles Melville Hays, commissioned it in 1907 and it was completed in 1912. He envisioned the Château Laurier as the flagship hotel of his railway and set off in 1912 to buy furnishings for it in Europe. Unfortunately, he decided to take the RMS *Titanic* on his way home. He and his party were just a few of the unfortunate souls who lost their lives when the *Titanic* went down.

However, Hays may have returned to see the opening of his hotel in June 1912 and may be taking care of it still. Hays was known as a whistler. That's right, whether it was because of nerves or just that he was a happy-go-lucky fellow, he was known for whistling much of the time. And as it turns out, there have been a great many instances when people at the hotel have reported the sounds of a mysterious whistler when no one else was around. Perhaps it was all in their own heads or perhaps they were unaware they were whistling themselves, but the famous Château Laurier whistler has been reported more than a few times.

Apparently Hays occasionally shows himself on the fifth floor as well. But mainly, he's known for whistling a jaunty tune. And it's not that famous melody about the *Titanic* sinking either.

The Château Laurier is located next to Parliament Hill in Ottawa.

GRAVENHURST OPERA HOUSE
GRAVENHURST

The Gravenhurst Opera House opened its doors in 1901. The imposing old theatre has served mainly as a theatrical house, but over the years, it's also hosted town council meetings, war rallies and court proceedings—and the old girl is apparently haunted. The ghost in question is referred to as "Ben," and he is thought to be the ghost of a lighting man who plunged to his death while working on some production. Will these theatre lighting guys never learn to use a crash mat? Anyway, Ben is said to be a relatively friendly fellow, though he likes to play jokes on occasion. Most of his jokes, not surprisingly, have to do with turning the lights on or off. Seems that even ghosts take their jobs home with them. Ben's also been known to do a tap dance, or it might just be the odd way he walks. If you'd like to meet Ben, he, like all lighting guys, is very busy, so you should make an appointment. Heck, why not just go see a show? The Gravenhurst Opera House is located at 295 Muskoka Road South in Gravenhurst.

BIG

GARGANTUAN & RIDICULOUSLY OVERSIZED

Shoe Tree

Although it's not unique to the Niagara region alone, the type of roadside attraction known as a "shoe tree" pops up from time to time in various places around the province. My friend Susan Ferrier-Mackay first told me about one such tree on the south side of Lakeshore Road (that's the right side) as you drive into Niagara-on-the-Lake from St. Catharines. But an even better shoe tree, with tons of shoes nailed to it, is located outside Fort Erie on Point Albino Road, just north of Highway 3. Thanks to Marissa Harvey, Marketing and Communications Services Coordinator with the Niagara Parks Commission, who directed me to that one and also clarified the purpose of the shoe trees as a practice "that gives families something creative to do with old shoes." Hey, why not? In Hamilton, all we did with old shoes was throw them out...or wear them because we couldn't afford new ones. This whole creative shoe tree practice just proves to me that people in the Niagara region are just like people in Alberta (as I found out while researching *Weird Canadian Places*). They're all just wacky to the core!

CANADIAN MUSEUM OF NATURE
OTTAWA

The castle-like Canadian Museum of Nature is located at the corner of Metcalf and Macleod Streets in downtown Ottawa. It's our country's own natural history museum. Hands-on exhibits include everything to do with plants, animals and dinosaurs.

The museum is housed in the Victoria Memorial Museum building, which was the temporary home of Parliament from 1916–18 after the original Parliament Buildings burned down. The body of Prime Minister Wilfrid Laurier lay in state here after he died. The architecture of the building is supposed to mirror that of the centre block of Parliament, so it's all high ceilings, stained glass and carved wood. You know, like museums used to be—scary. So it's no surprise that the museum is thought to be haunted. All sorts of ghostly goings-on have been reported there. Heck, the staff have even been known to point out the ghostly sites to interested members of the public.

The fourth floor of the building seems to be where a lot of ghostly stuff happens, including the sighting of a mysterious shadowy figure, lights going on and off, and alarms sounding for no reason. Trouble-making kids haven't been entirely ruled out, though. There are also reports of artifacts moving askew, vacuum cleaners being mysteriously unplugged and elevators deciding by themselves what floors they'd like to visit. No one likes a pushy elevator. Am I wrong? Anyway, the museum is a weird and fun place to visit whether you're in the market for a little spook'em up or not.

THE GREAT AND FREAKY OUTDOORS

The great outdoors seems to be a perfectly fine place to haunt, especially if you're a ghost who likes fresh air...or has a bit of asthma, I guess. The ghosts who favour the outdoors have a real creative spirit about them, too. These ghosts will mimic a motorcycle, paddle a canoe, fire their cannons, lurk near a lighthouse, traipse a former battlefield and, of course, hang out in a cemetery. There really are not a lot of restrictions to creeping out the great outdoors, so here are my favourite outdoor ghosts!

SCUGOG ISLAND

An hour's drive northeast of Toronto, near Port Perry, lies Scugog Island in Lake Scugog. Lake Scugog and the island were created when a dam was built at Purdy's Mills (now called Lindsay) in 1827. The lake covers 100 km². The island is mostly rural, though it's large enough to have farms and villages on it.

And with that rural area comes the story of a lonely and desolate island road where a legend of woe has grown up.

The isolated road is where a motorcyclist is supposed to have died and whose phantom continues to ride and haunt with vim, vigour and speed today. Oh, and not much skill, since the accident that killed him in the first place in the 1950s or 1960s keeps stopping him in his tracks.

The legend says that the kid in question was trying out a motorcycle on a straight road, misjudged his speed, lost control, flew off the bike and hit his head on a rock. Oh, and he died. Considering the type of crash, his driving skills can clearly be brought into question. Anyway, he apparently won't leave and making fun of him is probably not going to help.

This modern haunting phenomenon takes the form of a round, white light (which looks like a motorcycle headlight) that travels down the road and becomes a small red light when it passes you. So, headlight in one direction and brake light in the other direction. Got it? Some people have even suggested that they've heard the sound of a motorcycle engine along with the sight of the lights. They later had their hearing checked, but nothing was found, so they had their heads examined—still nothing!

Psychics, paranormal researchers and even reporters have examined the phenomenon. Explanations range from the reflection of car headlights, lights caused by a nearby geological fault and a complete and utter hoax. Still, people who have been there swear there is something to the ghostly lights of the poor and unskilled phantom motorcycle-riding kid! Vroom, vroom!

CANOE LAKE
ALGONQUIN PROVINCIAL PARK

Algonquin Provincial Park is the second oldest provincial park in Canada. Bet you didn't expect a history lesson at this point, huh? Established in 1893, the park covers 7723 km²—that's larger than Prince Edward Island...and a lot less sandy. The vast park includes numerous woodlands, lakes and rivers and is situated on the south edge of the Canadian Shield between Georgian Bay and the Ottawa River. Algonquin is remote, easy to get lost in and full of stories that include ghosts, murder and mystery.

And that's how we come to Tom Thompson. His death and what followed have become one of the best examples of Algonquin's mysterious lore.

For the ghost of Tom Thomson haunts Canoe Lake in Algonquin Park. That's right! The late and venerated painter of the Canadian wilderness and affiliate of the Group of Seven—but not a member, because he, like Groucho Marx later, would never join any club that would have him as a member...or something like that...

We all remember the story forced on us in history or art class where they talked about how old T.T. was an accomplished out-doorsman and talented painter, right? You know, the one where they told us that somehow in 1917, T.T. turned up dead on Canoe Lake under his canoe with a gash on his head and fishing line wrapped around his ankle. I don't know about you, but I am clearly seeing an ironic Mister Bean–like moment that, if it weren't so tragic, would actually be sitcom funny.

Anyway, since 1917, people claim to have seen a lone and ghostly figure paddling his canoe across Canoe Lake through the mist. He's always identified as T.T. because he's kind of a benign haunter. He doesn't say anything to anyone or scare them or even do a quick sketch that they could sell to the National Gallery for a fin or a million. He just paddles... paddles...paddles.

Explanations for T.T.'s mysterious death include a love triangle gone wrong—oh, you know those artists. There's also some con-troversy surrounding the fact that his family had him moved from his original burial site beside Canoe Lake to Heath, Ontario. Claims have been made that some other body—perhaps aboriginal—showed up in T.T.'s Canoe Lake grave in the 1950s.

STRATFORD

Stratford is a very pleasant rural town renowned for its theatre festival of the same name. It's quiet for the most part, though there is a bit of hullabaloo while the actors are in town in summer acting their little hearts out.

Before theatre-related tourism became the mainstay of Stratford, it was a sleepy farming community. But not that sleepy, for in the 1870s, the body of a dead man was found floating in Stratford's Avon River in a casket, but without a head.

The "real" explanation is that a local medical student needed a cadaver to practise on, so he dug up a body and did his practising. Not sure what happened to the head of the poor dead guy or what kind of practising the med student was doing on the body. Perhaps it was an early brain transplant? Or spinal surgery? Or a neckopathy?

What I really want to know is, did the medical student pay a fine for his dastardly, though educational deed or did he go to jail or ever become a doctor? Perhaps only the headless corpse knows for sure, because ever since that day, a headless ghost has haunted the banks of the Avon River. He rides up and down and back and forth looking for his head—which you can imagine is quite difficult if you don't have eyes...or a head in which to put them.

DAN'S OWN GHOST STORY: THE HAUNTED HOUSE OF HESTER STREET

HAMILTON

I think every kid knows of some structure in the neighbourhood that is identified as haunted. For me, growing up in Hamilton, the structure was a house that stood at the southwest corner of Manning and Hester Streets on Hamilton's mountain. When I was a grade school student at Ridgemount Public School, I passed that house just about every day. It was simply known to all of us kids as the "haunted house." It was two storeys high and, I think, some kind of split-level place. The images I have in my mind about that house involve it being devoid of colour—dark, mysterious and life-sucking. It had broken windows all around. The front door was sometimes ajar and at other times sealed up tight. This just added to the idea of ghosts coming and going in that spooky old place. I'd heard stories of kids going into that house and having the wits scared out of them—even stories about kids entering, but never leaving. People talked about these incidents, but no names or confirmation of the events were ever available. But that didn't matter—the house was evil! And as I later found out, with most ghost stories and haunted houses, confirmation is elusive—and unnecessary.

Our haunted house had become possessed, so kid folklore said, when the youngest son of the family murdered his parents. Apparently the place still ran with blood, which of course kept drying up and making the house darker and more evil. One day, someone dared me to go into that house, so I had to try. I mean, it was a dare, right?

After meandering my way to the house with a group of friends, I slowly made my way across the overgrown lawn. I lifted my right foot onto the porch and began putting my weight on it. I continued slowly, focused on my movements, hearing every bit of breath as it filled my lungs, until...the floorboard creaked with the ferocity of a blood-curdling scream. So, I turned tail and ran like a little girl going home for lunch. I never ever got that close to the "haunted house" again. It was then, and still remains for me today, the weirdest place I've ever been.

Oh, and by the way, I was never so surprised when as an adult, I went back to Hamilton and discovered that the "haunted house" was occupied—by humans. The whole place had been transformed into a brightly coloured suburban home where a family lived. A manicured lawn and a car in the driveway were its great new assets. It was a shocker. I wanted to go up to the door and ask the occupants if they knew what evil had occupied that house before they moved in. But the place still scared the bejeezes out of me. Bright paint and a freshly cut lawn couldn't take that type of evil away.

BIG
GARGANTUAN &
RIDICULOUSLY
OVERSIZED

Husky the Muskie

At 3 metres in height, "Husky the Muskie," that venerable mascot of Kenora, still flings himself high over the town's harbour front. Well, he's stationary, but he looks like he's jumping out of the water or flinging himself onto a barbeque. Anyway, Kenora's 1966 centennial project has been bringing people to the town for more than 40 years now, or so they say. Now, I wonder how many more years of magic he's got left in him?

A Crater, a Ring
or an Occasional
Glowing Orb

Some places transcend time, leap across the ages and con-
nect the past with our future. Some do not. Of course, this
chapter will deal with weird Ontario places that I have
determined transcend, leap or connect. The ones that
don't do at least two of these three things have been booted.
Perhaps for them, there is still slim hope for sainthood or
a seat in the Senate.

Some of Ontario's weirdest places are, alas, no longer with
us because of neglect, the former Mike Harris government
or simply because a mall has to be built somewhere.
I mean, people have to consume, right? These fascinating,
and in some cases really old, sites are relegated to pictures
and memories and remembrances of better times. (Cue
the violins.) However, their impact on the weirdness that
is Ontario is not lost, forgotten or diminished. That is, if
I have anything to say about it!

AUTOHENGE
OSHAWA

Like the dawn of a new age, Autohenge rose on the grassy knoll of a farmer's field one morning way back in 1986. It was conceived and built by a then-rising-star artist, environmentalist and true original, Bill Lishman. A farmer's field north of Oshawa was the setting for the full-scale replica of the infamous Salisbury Plain monument, except that this replica was built out of partially crushed cars as opposed to the original's sarsen and bluestones.

Chrysler Canada used the monument in advertising to illustrate the fate of their rivals' cars. The sculptor took old cars, placed them vertically and crushed them slightly to create the familiar circular ring of Stonehenge. He then used more cars horizontally to cap some of the verticals to create a full-sized copy of the "Henge" that included the familiar post-and-lintel arrangement.

Autohenge existed for five years and attracted tourists from around the world. According to Bill Lishman, an extraordinary number of people experienced a profound sense of déjà vu while visiting Autohenge. I always get misty around old cars, myself. Lishman says Autohenge déjà vu happened to him the day they completed the sculpture.

On that afternoon in 1986, when the structure was completed, Lishman remembers there was an impending electrical storm. He says he looked up at one moment to see the hair on all four of the people working on the site "standing straight out like dandelions gone to seed." Frightened by the sight, Lishman and his workers hightailed it out of the Oshawa 'Henge site in a hurry. A neighbour later reported seeing a lightning strike within Autohenge's ring that very afternoon. Was it coincidence, a spooky mystery or a godly form of disapproval? You be the judge.

Sadly, Autohenge was dismantled in the early 1990s, and nothing is left except a subtle ring that sometimes shows in the crops that are grown on the knoll. The farmer who owned the land became worried about liability, and according to Bill Lishman: "Autohenge fell to the fear of those dark minions of Satan who might arrange blame on him for some perceived happening." Translation—it had become the site for moonlit teenage druid events—a spot where teenage girls sacrificed their virginity by night and others could supplement their incomes during the day by gathering up empty beer bottles from the previous night's festivities.

Bill Lishman went on to create an ice version of Stonehenge called Icehenge on Lake Scugog as well as many other sculptures and an underground dwelling. You can find out more about this Canadian original at www.williamlishman.com.

SUPER CONNIE'S AIRPLANE BAR
MISSISSAUGA

What a concept! You take a beloved old passenger plane, anchor it to the ground, build wooden steps leading up to its doors fore and aft and serve drinks to people who gather inside. If this isn't the height of kitsch, I don't know what is. And that's what they did at Toronto's Pearson Airport.

The plane in question is a Lockheed Super Constellation, and these planes are beyond beloved. Four propellers, a black nose, three rudders—sleek mid-century design. This one previously flew with Trans-Canada Airlines (TCA), the forerunner of Air Canada, and is the last of TCA's Super Connies. In fact, it's the last Super Constellation in Canada (more on that later). Howard Hughes more or less designed this plane for TWA, where he was the controlling shareholder from 1939 to 1966. Most of the world's major airlines flew these planes in the 1940s and 1950s. They were also known as Starliners.

Super Connie's Airplane Bar never really took off as a fine dining establishment or even a popular hangout. The kindest words I've heard about the restaurant/bar are that the beer was cold! After it opened in 1998, business dropped off, and finally, in 2002, the plane as restaurant/bar closed its doors for good.

Now it looks as though Super Connie's Airplane Bar will never fly again as either a bar or a plane or as a Canadian-owned piece of aviation history. At press time, Super Connie's had been dismantled and the plane moved to a hangar down the road, where it's awaiting new paint that will restore it to its original TCA colours and design. The Museum of Flight in Seattle, Washington, bought the plane, and it was supposed to have been shipped there already. But the tangled web that is the life of Super Connie's is not over—it's gotten more tangled. Many people involved in Canadian aviation are vocally opposed to our last beloved Super Connie being moved to the United States.

The Toronto Aerospace Museum has been trying to acquire the Super Connie in question for its collection since 2001. Now they have been joined by the Air Canada Pionairs (a group of 12,000 retirees from Air Canada and affiliated airlines), and both organizations are urging the federal government to have Super Connie's designated as "moveable cultural property" and to not issue an export permit. This would keep the plane from being exported to the United States or any other country.

Well, as they say, it's not over until the last airplane cocktail swizzle stick has swizzled. The government has yet to make a decision on the cultural property issue or the export permit.

Either way, the absolutely unique airplane bar concept seems to be sunk. You definitely won't be able to see the Super Connie at its former location, the intersection of Derry Road East and Torbram Road in Mississauga. Most likely, you'll have to visit the United States to see it, though there is still hope that with enough public outcry (hint, hint), the bar may fly again on Canadian soil...or the plane may bar again!

CAMP X
WHITBY

Moonless nighttime parachute drops, slipping past armed guards, making your way through locked doors, silently sneaking up on your enemy, cold-blooded killing, slipping away without a trace, blowing things up with plastic explosives, evading capture and ultimately being captured and withstanding torture... Ahh, the life of a spy—and the realities of living, teaching and training at Camp X.

Camp X was, of course, a top-secret World War II Allied training base for spies. It was built on the shores of Lake Ontario by a Winnipeg-born industrialist named Sir William Stephenson at the request of British Prime Minister Winston Churchill. "The Man Called Intrepid," as Churchill codenamed Stephenson, chose 105 hectares of land on the borders of Whitby and

Oshawa as the site of the base. The location was chosen because it was far from the enemy, easily concealed from the locals and close to the United States. And probably dirt cheap!

Officially known by British Security Coordination (BSC) as Special Training School 103 (STS 103), Camp X was set up in 1941. In fact, it opened on December 6, 1941. The following day, December 7, 1941, the Japanese attacked Pearl Harbor and the Americans entered World War II. What's up with that weird coincidence? Or is it a coincidence?

Throughout the war, the base trained agents from all over the world—the French, Poles, Hungarians, Italians and even a few Anglos. They became experts in sabotage, subversion, deception, wireless operation and intelligence gathering. After agents completed their training, instructors assessed their abilities and individuals were sent to Britain, where assignments were made. Soon after that, agents were dropped behind enemy lines. It's been estimated that more than 500 agents were trained at Camp X and fewer than half of them survived the war, though some of Camp X's successful spies went on to continue their activities during the Cold War. Isn't it good to know that some of these veteran spies were able to put their wartime training to use after the war?

Along with training spies in the more covert operations of war, Camp X was the command centre for Hydra, a radio network that communicated vital information between Canada, the United States, South America and Britain. Hydra was created, for the most part, by a group of amateur Canadian radio enthusiasts.

Some of the more famous people to have passed through Camp X include: Ian Fleming, the creator of James Bond; Wild Bill Donovan, the man who set up American's Office of Strategic Services (the forerunner of the CIA); Igor Gouzenko, the Russian cipher who defected to Canada and was held at Camp X under protective custody in 1945; and British author Roald Dahl, whose observations about activities at Camp X were used in a manual that was intended to be a blueprint for British Intelligence operations. (Do people still wonder where he got his ideas for *Charlie and the Chocolate Factory* and *James and the Giant Peach*? Come on, people!)

Not so strangely, there is virtually nothing left of the original Camp X. Apparently spies don't like to leave traces of themselves or their work behind. A monument was built on the original site and dedicated in 1984 by Ontario's lieutenant-governor, John Black Aird. It overlooks the lake in what is now called Intrepid Park and consists of four flagpoles and a cairn with two plaques on it. The first plaque is dedicated to the men and women who served at Camp X. It reads:

> CAMP X
> *1941–1946*
> *On this site British Security Co-ordination operated special training school No. 103 and HYDRA.*
> *STS 103 trained Allied agents in the techniques of secret warfare for the Special Operations Executive (SOE) branch of the British Intelligence Service.*
> *Hydra network communicated vital messages between Canada, the United States and Great Britain.*
> *This commemoration is dedicated to the service of the men and women who took part in these operations.*

A second, smaller plaque is dedicated to Intrepid himself. It reads:

> *In memory of*
> *Sir William Stephenson*
> *"The Man Called Intrepid"*
> *Born at Winnipeg, Canada, January 11, 1896*
> *Died at Paget, Bermuda, January 31, 1989*
> *Director of British Security Co-ordination*
> *1941–1946*

Lynn Philip Hodgson, the author of a book entitled *Inside Camp X*, conducts tours of the former facility by request. On his website (http://webhome.idirect.com/~lhodgson/campx.htm), he says that original Camp X artifacts can still be found there along the shores of the lake. If you hurry, I'm sure you'll find some concrete that was blown to pieces or an old spark plug or two. The Camp X Historical Society (http://www.campxhistoricalsociety.ca/) has many artifacts in its possession and is currently trying to raise money to build a museum on the Camp X site.

Intrepid Park and the Camp X monument are located at Boundary Road, south of Wentworth Avenue and the LCBO store in Whitby.

BIG GARGANTUAN & RIDICULOUSLY OVERSIZED

Photo-Mosaic

The "World's Largest Permanent Historical Photo-Mosaic" (now that's a mouthful) covers a wall of the old Hannah's grocery store building overlooking the locks in Port Carling in Muskoka. The mural was officially unveiled on Simcoe Day in 2005 by Ontario Lieutenant-Governor James K. Bartleman and was designed to commemorate Port Carling's 100-year anniversary (1860–1960). "The Wall," as it is amiably referred to, is made up of thousands of historical postcards dating back to 1860. They were collected from locals, including the lieutenant-governor's mother, and arranged to create a scene 34 metres wide by 14 metres tall. The scene shows the steamboat RMS *Sagamo* passing through the Port Carling locks.

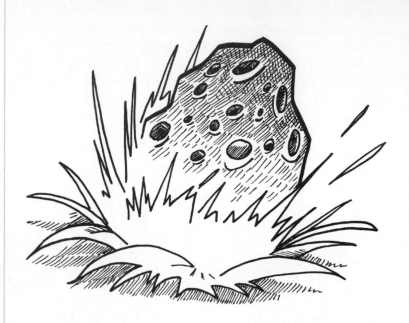

HOLLEFORD METEOR CRATER
NEAR HARTINGTON (NORTH OF KINGSTON)

If you had been standing on what is known as the Babcock Homestead Farm 550 million years ago, boy would you have had a shock! First off, you couldn't have been standing there, because humans didn't yet exist. In fact, you'd most likely be algae. You know, a one-celled or multicellular rootless plant that typically grows in water. You'd probably look like pond scum. That would have been a shock to you, I'm sure. But more shocking would have been the sight of a 90-metre-in-diameter meteorite barrelling towards you at 55,000 kilometres per hour. Just how fast is that? Well, running wouldn't have done any good, and not just because you didn't have legs. Not even the Six Million Dollar Man or Ben Johnson on steroids could run away that fast. That's faster than any military plane or any rocket or any vehicle "officially" known to man today. It's really, really, really, really fast!

Now, we all remember from our high-school science classes what a meteorite is, right? Anyone? Well, I looked it up, just in case you're not sure. According to NASA, a meteorite is "a solid body that has arrived on the Earth or Moon from outer space. It can range in size from microscopic to many tonnes. Its composition ranges from that of silicate rocks to metallic iron-nickel." In ordinary language, it's a big chunk of rock or metal that plows into the Earth from space—but isn't an Earth-impacting human-made space vehicle, which is good!

On that day, or night, 550 million years ago, you would have seen (if only pond scum had eyes) the Holleford Meteorite, which caused the Holleford Meteor Crater, approaching from the north. A bow wave of air would have ripped open the countryside. If you'd had ears, the noise would have ruptured them before tearing them off. Before the meteorite actually struck the Earth and its pond scum inhabitants, the bow wave dug out a huge valley more than 2 kilometres wide. Then finally, the meteorite smashed into the earth, causing a huge mushroom cloud of crud (including pond scum and terra firma) to fly into the air. The resulting impact left a crater 250 metres deep and 2.5 kilometres wide. Now that, my friends, would make some amusement park simulator ride, don't you think? I can see it now. Ride a meteorite into the Earth—a joint Disney-ILM production. (But hands off, Disney guys, copyright is mine!)

Back to Holleford. Soon after the impact, the crater became a lake. Still later, the Palaeozoic seas swept through, brought sediment with them, and filled the crater to its current depth of 30 metres. So, like a CIA or Camp X operation, everything was covered up.

And a good job nature did of covering it up. The crater and its explosive story weren't discovered until 1955. That's when the

Canadian government began aerial mapping of the region, using techniques that were developed during World War II. The aerial photographs revealed the possible existence of the impact crater. Further studies have proved the theory.

At the site of the impact (about a half-hour drive north of Kingston), the Ontario government erected a commemorative plaque along the road beside the Babcock Homestead Farm. There isn't much evidence of the impact unless you're scientist, a dreamer or look really close and have a wild and/or demented imagination. Standing near the sign, you can tell you're in a valley. Certainly for most of us that wouldn't be nary a clue to being in an impact crater. But if you look towards the north, squint like you're looking at a piece of "Magic Eye" art and perhaps stand on one leg, you can kind of almost see the valley pathway that was carved by the bow wave of the meteorite.

There is a reason the Holleford Meteor Crater is in this chapter about things that are gone, but not forgotten. Basically, to any ordinary person, there isn't much to see here. But it's wild to think about what once was, right? There are, in fact, other meteor impact craters in Ontario (Sudbury got all its nickel from a meteorite impact), but believe it or not, Holleford is about the easiest one to see.

The exact location is 44°27.511' N, 076°37.985' W. Hope this helps!

BIG
GARGANTUAN &
RIDICULOUSLY
OVERSIZED

Big Joe Muffraw

Beside the Mattawa Museum at Explorer's Point in Mattawa is a 5-metre-tall statue of a lumberjack with an axe, all carved from a whole mess o' pine. The statue is a tribute to a real-life folk hero named Big Joe Muffraw or Muffaraw or Mufferaw or Montferrand.... "Big Joe," as we'll call him, was a French Canadian lumberjack who worked the Ottawa River in the mid-19th century. He was apparently born in Montréal and died in 1864, and his tough reputation went before him, whereas behind him he left his heel print and name carved into the ceilings of the bars he visited. Big Joe may also have worked in the United States and be the real-life version of Paul Bunyan. Over the years, the stories about Big Joe have been embellished, expanded and stretched to their maximum. There have been books written about him, but he's probably most famous because of the mid-1970s Stompin' Tom Connors song "Big Joe Mufferaw." The statue in Mattawa is the last of 23 historical figures created out of wood in the Mattawa-Bonfield region.

Gruesome, Ghoulish
and a Bit Foolish

In this chapter, we offer up some of Ontario's weirdest places in terms of the macabre, the gruesome and the ghoulish. If you're really up for some weird treats, you can tour the home of a murdered Irish family in Biddulph, head down the road and visit their gravesite or perhaps wait along the Roman Line for a headless horseman to say "hello." I'm not exactly sure how a headless horseman says hello, but I've been told that the ghost of Annie Sullivan has also visited the area.

In this chapter, you'll also find a funhouse in Niagara Falls that I don't think is much fun; an Ottawa Hostel that's pretty hostile; a hermitage with a couple of hermits; and a Guilded Inn where the guild has worn off.

So if you dare,
Go right ahead,
Visit these gems,
Don't lose your head.
For whether they're gruesome,
Or whether they're ghoulish,
If you choose to visit them,
You must be foolish...

THE DONNELLY HOMESTEAD
BIDDULPH TOWNSHIP

Some people might call it the enterprising idea of a smart entrepreneur who saw a need and filled it. Others would call it macabre, gruesome, ghoulish, sick, scary and in bad taste. I have a feeling that, either way, the publicity is welcome and the business thrives.

We're talking about a business that highlights, celebrates and even exploits the massacre of five members of an Irish immigrant family. Now, if it was a recent massacre, I'm sure the ghoulishness of it all would be much more in question. However, because it happened in 1880. I guess the time factor allows the macabre exploitation to seem, well...less exploitative. And to be fair, Robert Salts, who owns the Donnelly Homestead and runs the tour, isn't the first person to latch onto the Donnelly story and turn it into some form of economic gain.

Let's start at the beginning. On February 4, 1880, five members of an Irish immigrant family are murdered in a blood-soaked massacre in the early morning hours of. Killed in the melee are patriarch James Donnelly, his wife Johannah, sons Tom and John and niece Bridget, and the house is burned to the ground in the massacre. The known murderers are neighbours and town rivals of the Donnellys. There's an eyewitness to the massacre, but no one is ever convicted. And so the myth surrounding the events grows and grows until there's a bit of a book industry around it and a whole niche market involving more than just a few people.

And now there's a 90-minute tour of the former homestead of the murdered family. The tour apparently includes a look at artifacts, photographs and a tour of the "Donnelly barn." Of course, the original barn burned down and the one in the tour was built after the murders, but that doesn't stop it from being a tour highlight—no matter how irrelevant. You see, Salts thinks the barn is haunted.

I wonder if the tour contains moments like: "We think this is where Tom was pitch-forked" or "This is thought to be where Johannah swore vengeance on the murderers and took a last puff of her pipe."

Ghostly happenings surrounding the homestead have also been reported, including the murdered family materializing, horses being spooked and horses dying as a result of travelling the Roman Line (so named for the numerous Roman Catholic families who lived there) on the anniversary of the massacre. Talk about being tough on the animals! There's also an unsubstantiated (are you surprised?) report of a headless ghost that rides up and down the Roman Line. I guess you can wait around after the tour and see if he'll stop and talk or wave to you, or else you can head on down to St. Patrick's Church and view the dead family's gravestone. That's got to be a hoot!

The Donnelly Homestead site is located in Biddulph Township near Lucan, halfway between London and Exeter.

Avro Arrow

A large (but still scale) model of the legendary Canadian-designed-and-built fighter aircraft, the Avro Arrow, is located in Zurakowski Park across the street from the railway station in Barry's Bay. And just why would a replica of the mysteriously cancelled, ahead-of-its-time, legendary and infamous Canadian fighter be located in Barry's Bay, you ask? Because the principal test pilot of the Arrow, Janusz Zurakowski (pronounced Yanoosh Zurakovski), was a long-time resident of the town, that's why! And I can't think of a better reason. The ¼-scale replica of the supersonic, delta-wing interceptor is 6.7 metres long and has a wingspan of 3.8 metres. The park, the replica Arrow and a statue of Janusz Zurakowski were dedicated on July 26, 2003. In attendance at the ceremony were Arrow enthusiasts, Canadian Armed Forces personnel, the ambassador of Poland and the 88-year-old Janusz Zurakowski himself. Unfortunately, "Zura" died in 2004, before a museum showcasing artifacts about him and the CF-105 (that's the official designation of the Avro Arrow) could be added to the park. However, money is currently being raised for the museum and plans are moving ahead. Let's hope shaming a few levels of government might be part of that plan. Barry's Bay is located at the intersections of Highways 60 and 62 south, about 70 kilometres north of Bancroft.

CLIFTON HILL
NIAGARA FALLS

This one definitely fits into gruesome, ghoulish and especially FOOLISH! And this time I'm talking about the Canadian city of Niagara Falls and not the wonder of the world. Clifton Hill is the grand central terminal of tacky fun in the town. The part of the street I'm talking about runs from Falls Avenue to Victoria Avenue. It's quite a steep street. Your legs will notice you've been walking when you get to the top of the hill. Heck, even before you get partway up, you'll know you've been on an incline...an incline to hell!

And that's where the gruesome, ghoulish and foolish come in. Along this "Avenida de la Tacky," you'll find three attractions that cater particularly to people bent on being scared, frightened, grossed out and parted from their money.

Closest to the bottom of the Hill (the Falls Avenue end) is the "Haunted House." Mainly, this lowbrow attraction has dark halls—you're constantly waiting for something to jump out and scare the hair from your scalp. The fear of what's coming up is worse than most of what you see in the Haunted House. There are motion sensor buzzers and air jets and a few tacky monsters behind screens that light up when you go by.

The next attraction on the Hill is "Drakula's Haunted Castle." Again, there are the requisite dark hallways and fear-inducing "what's around the corner?" deals. But worst of all, there are people dressed up in monster suits that will jump out of the shadows, scare you and even touch you. Not inappropriately, but definitely in a scary way.

The final tacky and macabre attraction on the Hill is the "House of Frankenstein," and it is the worst in terms of gruesome. In here, you'll find darkened halls, uneven floors and other places lit by blacklight. There are scary creatures behind glass, Frankenstein's very scary lab and, worst of all, a torture chamber that will scare all but the bravest—and even some of them.

The final and tackiest of the area attractions is more than gruesome and ghoulish and is not actually on the Hill—it's just off the Hill on Victoria Street and is called the "Criminals Hall of Fame." As a kid, this one scared me to no end. As an adult, it is horribly gruesome and gaudy beyond anything I've ever seen, even in Las Vegas and Blackpool, England—and I've seen Siegfried and Roy. Ahhhhhhhhh!

The Criminals Hall of Fame has wax renditions of all of your favourite killers—if you have favourite killers, that is. From Al Capone and Adolph Hitler to Jeffrey Dahmer, Charles Manson and John Wayne Gacy, you can see them all here. You can even see some of the gruesome group in mid-crime. I won't go into which ones, because it is beyond bad taste, gruesome, ghoulish and really, really creepy.

The final nail in the coffin for the Criminals Hall of Fame is an electric chair, where you can sit and get a bit of a buzz while pretending to be executed. Your family and friends can also snap souvenir photos of your tacky faux execution. I wonder which of the next generation of serial killers will one day show up having had his photo taken in this spot and blame it for leading him to his ultimate demise?

I have to say, this one is just too much! Weird does not do it justice!

BIG
GARGANTUAN &
RIDICULOUSLY
OVERSIZED

Skating Rink

The world's largest skating rink can be found each year on Ottawa's Rideau Canal—in winter, that is. In summer, hip waders or water wings would be more appropriate than ice skates. For 36 years, the Rideau Canal has been serving up 7.8 kilometres of icy fun, officially called the Rideau Canal Skateway. The ice surface is equal to 90 Olympic skating rinks and it usually opens in late December and closes in early March. Oh, and triple Salchows are encouraged.

HI-OTTAWA
OTTAWA

The youth hostel at 75 Nicholas Street in Ottawa is a double whammy, first for its gruesome and ghoulish building, and second, for the fact that it is haunted. That's right, not content with having young people and adventurers alike staying in the converted cells of the former Carleton County Gaol (Jail), the hostellers will tell you straight out to expect weird and ghostly happenings.

Located in downtown Ottawa, the hostel is an imposing stone structure. Funny how jails were built as imposing structures. The jail opened its doors in 1862 and didn't close them until 1972. A year later, they were again opened after some renovation, and the former jail has been serving as a hostel ever since. The hostel is the perfect jumping-off point to explore the historic

capital city with all its museums and finery. "Jumping-off point" may be the key phrase as well, since the jail was the site of a few legally sponsored hangings and perhaps a great many more illegal ones. At this hostel, you can actually see where the executions took place. You can also visit the solitary confinement area and death row jail cells, which have been kept pretty much as they were when they were used to confine the unfortunate and the soon-to-be dead.

The least frightening of the jail/hostel's ghostly happenings involves a shower room, where you are more likely than not to emerge from cleansing your body to find that your clothes have been scattered every which way. Apparently, the ghost that haunts this part of the former jail hates neatly piled clothing and isn't afraid to show it.

Far more frightening (actually terrifying to me) is the ghost of Patrick James Whelan, who is said to still be a resident here despite having been hanged way back in 1869. Whelan was the convicted killer of Thomas D'Arcy McGee, who was a Father of Confederation and the only victim of political assassination in Canada's history. Whelan claimed he was innocent right up to the end—and a lot of good that did him! They hanged him anyway, and 5000 people came to see it.

Whelan's ghost has been seen, felt and even perhaps heard "hanging" around his death row cell. He has apparently been seen writing at a desk, holding his head in sorrow, and heard reciting the Lord's Prayer. I don't know about you, but I am never going to visit this place.

There are still more sprightly apparitions and sounds, including women screaming, children crying and mysterious banging noises. There may even be some sort of vampire lurking about. So, if gruesome is a keyword when you're looking for fine accommodation, head over to Ottawa's youth hostel. As for me, I'll have nightmares for weeks just thinking about it.

THE HERMITAGE
ANCASTER

The Hermitage is an almost legendary residence that was built in the old town of Ancaster. Ancaster was long a bedroom community to Hamilton, until it was amalgamated with Hamilton in 2001. Located on Sulphur Springs Road, the Hermitage site has been built on since the 1830s. One of the early owners was a Presbyterian minister named George Sheed. In its heyday, the Hermitage house included a library, drawing room, dining room, kitchen, nursery, laundry rooms and a carriage room. It was a swanky, happening place! Over the years, additions were made to the Hermitage, including a barn, granary buildings and a tenant farmer's residence.

The Hermitage changed owners a number of times, became an inn at one point and suffered more than a few fires. In 1934, the house finally burned to the ground when a fire raged through it during a party thrown by its owner, Mrs. Alma Dick-Lauder. Apparently, it wasn't a house warming, but it did end up being a warm house.

The elderly woman loved the house and refused to leave the site after the tragedy. She set up a tent on-site and lived there with her partially paralyzed dog while a smaller shelter was built inside the ruins. She died there in the late 1940s. No word on what happened to Rex the incredible paralyzed dog, though.

The ruin changed hands a few more times before finally being sold to the Hamilton and Region Conservation Authority, who are the current overseers.

Ghostly happenings at the Hermitage have been reported since at least the 1940s. The rather benign ghost of Mrs. Dick-Lauder is seen in the ruins from time to time. She's sometimes heard to ask for a match... Not really, but she is said to be looking for her dog, Rex... Not really, again. She actually just refuses to leave the home she loved so dearly. Awwww, that's nice.

There is another ghost on hand at the Hermitage, and he is much scarier. He is said to be the spirit of a former coachman. I haven't been able to uncover which tenant he was a coachman for or exactly why he hanged himself or if he did, in fact, hang himself, as the legend goes. However, he has been accused of scaring many a visitor to the Hermitage by appearing and approaching them with his hangman's noose clasped in his hand. Perhaps he just wants some help getting the knot out of the rope? Who knows for sure?

I've actually been to the Hermitage on many an occasion in daytime, at night and even when sober. People in the area know that it is often used by younger folk as "party central"—an out-of-the-way drinking spot, in other words. I have to admit that I've never seen nor heard anything unusual. But don't let my experience stop you from visiting. You can go see the Hermitage on your own or join a guided tour by Haunted Hamilton Ghost Walks.

BIG

GARGANTUAN & RIDICULOUSLY OVERSIZED

Snowman

The "World's Largest Snowman"—not actually made of the very real, very perishable and easily melting unstable precipitate known as snow—is located in Beardmore, near Lake Nipigon. At 10.7 metres tall, Beardmore's non-abominable snowman comes with removable seasonal accessories. He's like a giant GI Joe doll, I guess. In summer, Beardmore's snowguy sports sunglasses and a fishing pole; in winter, he's got a curling broom and a scarf. No word on spring or autumn attire, but I'm guessing something in leather couture from the dungeon-wear collection of Versace!

Monster Places
Not Affiliated with the
Discovery Channel

Monsters have been used throughout history to frighten children into not doing things their parents didn't want them to. You know the kind of thing I'm talking about: "Don't go near the water or the sea serpent will chew you to bits, Betsy." That kind of thing kept little Betsy and little Ben, but sadly not little Doug the Daring One, from going near shorelines and into lakes, oceans and other watery places where children might drown. In more modern and, dare I say it, enlightened times, swimming lessons help keep children from drowning. But to be fair, in medieval times and before ye olde peasants—the working poor and other non-sequitur descriptors meaning "the great unwashed masses"—hardly had the time or money to provide their little darlings with organized swimming lessons. I mean, they had backbreaking work to contend with in addition to tooth decay and their leaping leper parts falling into dung heaps. The last one, I believe is actually a Martha Stewart recipe.

☞

Anyway, despite the fact that we live in more enlightened times, monsters have stuck around, though less as tools of putting fear in children—except in Hamilton where I grew up and in lands ruled by right-wing political parties.

In big, old, brash and sophisticated Ontario, monsters continue to raise their ugly, misshapen, hairy, slimy, grotesque and occasionally cute heads. And then we laugh and we laugh and we laugh at the people who report back to us on them. Ontario has seen its share of monsters over the years, and some would say it continues to see them, though less frequently and with little fanfare. Near Cobalt, there's Old Yellow Top and Smithville has a half man–half beast, whatever that means. And then there are the water-logged creatures of the depths of our lakes: Kempenfelt Kelly and his alter ego Igopogo in Lake Simcoe; a trio known as the Great Snake, South Bay Bessie and the Erie Baby in Lake Erie; and near sleepy old Kingston, a slimy-headed creature dwells in the waters of Lake Ontario.

These are the places where you'll want to sit up and pay attention to view the shy monsters of Ontario.

LAKE SIMCOE
(44°25'00" N, 79°20'00" W)

Lake Simcoe is an hour's drive north of Toronto. It's an oval-shaped lake with a couple of irregular fingers that jut out north, south and west. The major city on Lake Simcoe is Barrie. The lake is known for offering much recreational activity and has a scary little secret—there's a lake monster there that, depending on where he's seen, goes either by the name "Igopogo" or "Kempenfelt Kelly." He's certainly not as famous as British Columbia's Ogopogo, though one of his names was definitely ripped off from that mysterious Lotus Land beast (or large dead log, depending on what you think of all this hoopla over lake creatures). And doesn't it just figure that Ontario needs two names for a creature that other provinces can name with just one? Perhaps if he wore a name tag, the mixup would be less pronounced.

As I said, Igopogo is simply Ogopogo with one different letter. Kempenfelt Kelly gets his name from Kempenfelt Bay, a place on the northwest side of the lake, where the creature has often been spotted. The creature also resembles Ogopogo in every aspect except one—he's actually quite tiny. Igopogo Kelly has been described as being no more than 3.5 metres in length and seems to move at a much more leisurely pace than other lake monsters. He's got a sense of humour, though, since many sightings involve him startling picnickers or sneaking up on unsuspecting boaters. Alcohol, I'm sure, had nothing to do with any of these encounters.

There's been speculation that Igofeltpogo Kelly is more mammalian than serpent-like. Infrequent sightings have also raised the possibility that IgoKelly-PogoFelt has passed on. Flags were flown at half-mast across the province last summer while suspiciously, "sea serpent" burgers were served all over Barrie.

BIG GARGANTUAN & RIDICULOUSLY OVERSIZED

Curling Stone

You'll find the "World's Largest Curling Stone" outside the Fort William Curling and Athletic Club in Thunder Bay. This curling stone rests, in a grand way, up high (low actually) on a pedestal. And just why shouldn't a curling stone be put on a pedestal? Well—look for my reasoning later in this section. The "rock" monument (to use the official curling lingo) to one of Canada's favourite "sports" stands 2 metres tall and has a diameter of 1.8 metres. It's also made of concrete, unlike the tinier, official stones, which are made from granite, weigh nearly 20 kilograms and measure about 28 centimetres in diameter. This giant curling stone has been in Thunder Bay since 1960, when it was created for that year's Brier. I know I'm going to get into trouble for this (not the least of which is going to come from my Nana), but for me, the fact that curling is such a hit in Canada has always been an embarrassment. I know, I know, people here just love it. I've even played the game, sport, sliding, spinning, bowling-like thingy hazard, or whatever else you want to call it. There is definitely skill involved, I give you that! But to me, it's still little more than shuffleboard on ice. I know, the letters are already being written. Canada wins international tournaments in curling, you'll tell me. We won a gold medal in Turin—I know, I know! But come on—it's so dull to watch! And I still have trouble with the fact that it's called a sport and not a pastime. To me, it's similar to darts. You know—the game that's played in pubs throughout the world. I say any game that can be played while drinking a pint isn't really a sport, but who am I to judge? By the way, if anyone knows where I can find a giant roadside attraction of a dart and dartboard, please let me know.

LAKE ONTARIO AT KINGSTON
(44°18'24" N, 76°24'59" W)

Kingston is located halfway between Canada's two largest cities: Goose Bay and Big-Joke-of-the-World. Of course, that is not correct. I just thought I'd throw in some misinformation to make sure you're paying attention. As we all know, Toronto and Montréal are Canada's largest cities and Kingston lies halfway between the two of them at the eastern end of that immense, one might say Great, Lake Ontario. The city is famous for its numerous prisons, Old Fort Henry, the Royal Military College and Queen's University (which is a royal reference, not an institution of higher learning exclusively for gay men), as well as for its water. Yes indeed, Kingston is a port city where boats abound. It's a major jumping-off point for cruising the Thousand Islands; each year it's the site of the Canadian Olympic Training Regatta; and it's also known for having some of the world's best freshwater shipwreck diving.

These are all enviable attractions, but none of them gets Kingston a listing in this chapter on monsters. What does get it that listing is a shy and unassuming winged water beast that goes by the ultra-cutesy name of "Kingstie."

Kingstie is a wee spec of a lass when compared to the Nessies and Ogopogos of world lake-monster lore. However, do not underestimate her powers when it comes to drawing tourists and their shiny monetary trinkets to Kingston's shores in summer. She's not quite a cash cow yet, but they're working on her being a debit card carp!

Kingstie cuts a distinctive, if not murky or varied presence. She is said to be either 1.2 metres wide and 2.5 metres long or between 6 and 12 metres in length and eel-like. Kingstie may also have one or two eyes, antlers and a dripping mane that many think is a wig. Okay, it's just me that thinks it's a wig, but I ask you, how else could a famous lake monster avoid the paparazzi if she didn't occasionally don a disguise? Huh?

Sightings of Kingstie de Kingston date back 200 years, if you include all the various Lake Ontario sightings, which I do, since if she wasn't sighted in the Kingston area, Kingstie was probably visiting relatives or on vacation. I mean, what is the chance of there being more than one murky mystery of Lake Ontario's depths that wasn't dumped there by the Cosa Nostra, mutated because of a nuclear power plant or created out of Burlington Bay sludge? There's really no answer to that, is there? So, don't bother asking me what Kingstie really is. If you go back a few paragraphs, you can clearly figure out what I think.

LAKE ERIE
(42°27'15" N, 81°07'17" W)

Of the five Great Lakes, Erie is fourth in terms of its size (385 kilometres long, covering about 3021 km²). It's also the shallowest of the Greats (just 64 metres at its deepest point) and the smallest of the Greats by water volume, making it the warmest of the Greats in summer and often the only Great Lake to freeze over in the winter. As we should all know, Lake Erie forms a border between Ontario and four U.S. states: New York, Pennsylvania, Ohio and Michigan. Its shores are heavily urbanized (especially on the U.S. side), and in 1813, Lake Erie was the setting for a great naval victory by Commodore Oliver Hazard Perry over the British at Put-in-Bay. You get the point—Lake Erie is small compared to most of the other Great Lakes, but has lots of people and a bountiful history.

But let's not forget one other thing about Lake Erie: the Great Snake...or South Bay Bessie...or the very sketchy and clearly a hoax Erie Baby. That's right, these are just three of the names given to Lake Erie's monster of a mysterious underwater creature. One of these was clearly a hoax, the others...well, who knows?

For years, the Erie Baby was purported to be a metre-long baby plesiosaur that washed up on the beach in Ohio sometime in the early 1990s. As it turned out, the comedic lake creature in question was nothing more than a lawyerfish that a taxidermist modified to make look like a plesiosaur. There's always some sort of lawyer behind the lie, isn't there? The Erie Baby was purchased and displayed in a creationist museum in Texas for many years until the hoax was uncovered. An interesting thing to note about the hoax is that the original creator never tried to pretend that the Erie Baby was anything other than something created by him and not by a higher power.

Many sightings of the real Lake Erie creature have taken place on both sides of the border: at Crystal Beach and Lowbanks on the Ontario side and at Toledo, Sandusky and Vermilion on the American side. Many of the sightings have been reported at lakeside amusement parks on both sides of the border: Cedar Point at Sandusky, Ohio, and the former Crystal Beach amusement park in Ontario. Demonic connection or weird, wild coincidence? I don't know—perhaps the Erie creature is a Phantom of the Opera–type beast. Maybe it was the original inspiration for the many roller coasters once found at Crystal Beach and still found at Cedar Point. Or perhaps it just wants to have some fun and scare the bejeezes out of itself on a park ride? Will the world ever really know? Perhaps a highly skilled, motivated and determined team from *ET Canada* could investigate? Or they could continue doing what it is they do. What is it they do?

Anyway, on the U.S. side of the lake, the creature has been given the name "South Bay Bessie." Probably so they can keep track of it because they think it's an illegal. We don't have a great name for it on the Ontario side, except the "Great Snake." Great, really, just great.

The Bessie Snake, as I like to call it, is a relatively benign creature, often seen splashing about, rollicking in the waves or sunning itself. It's said to be dark brown, dark blue, black or green with white spots—some would suggest chameleon-like. It has between zero and five humps, at least one eye and is anywhere from 10 to 15 metres long.

I also hear the monster's willing to do a sit-down interview if it gets the questions in advance and monies are paid to its favourite charity, Save the Serpents.

BIG
GARGANTUAN &
RIDICULOUSLY
OVERSIZED

Hereford

A rather squat-looking (or stout or portly) giant Hereford bull statue can be found in Chesley on the front lawn of the municipal building on Bruce Road 10. Strangely enough, the portly beef big boy is named "Bruce" after the county in which he's found. That's Bruce County for those who haven't followed along. Anyway, Bruce is there proclaiming that Bruce County is the "Beef Capital of Ontario." It's an area that is apparently surrounded by some of the best beef cattle farms in Canada. After this entry, watch the letters roll in to Bruce County disputing their claim. As for me, I'm not judging the fine beef cattlemen in Bruce County or anywhere else. I am, however, enthralled by the big boy known as Bruce and wonder what kind of spectacular eatin' he'd make.

COBALT
(47°23'57" N, 79°40'50" W)

Cobalt is located halfway between North Bay and Kirkland Lake near Lake Timiskaming. The town has a population of about 1200 people, though in its silver-mining heyday, around 1910, it had a population of 10,000. The town takes its name from the metal that was mined in the area. However, it's best known for its silver mines, which at one time produced the fourth largest amount of silver in the world. The town has never quite recovered its glory days, though it was named Ontario's "Most Historic Town" by TV Ontario's current affairs show *Studio 2*. So, it's almost back, right?

Anyway, Cobalt is no stranger to rocks and metal and colourful names, so why should we be so surprised to find out there's a Bigfoot near Cobalt that goes by the name "Old Yellow Top"? Ah, say what? Oh no, it's true. But to be fair, when the creature was first sighted at the turn of the 20th century, he was called just "Yellow Top." Seems the adjective "Old" was added after World War II because he'd started looking a bit haggard.

Old Yellow Top (OYT for short) is said to stand nearly 2 metres tall on two legs and walk like a man. Does that mean he walks in a masculine, determined way as opposed to wiggling his hips like a female Bigfoot might? Anyway, his body is buff. Buff, buff, buff! Actually, we don't know that. All that's really been said about OYT's body is that it's entirely covered in black hair. His head is said to be covered in blond or light-coloured hair, which may extend down over his shoulders. That is, of course, where he gets his name. Hmmm? Covered in black hair, but blond on top? I'm thinking lost southern European individual who's into nudism but wants to be seen as more northern European so he dyes his head hair blond thinking no one will notice the discrepancy with his hair colour down below. Or maybe the sun has bleached his head hair that way naturally? Sure.

The last reported sighting of OYT was in the 1970s, when a busload of miners veered off the road to avoid him and almost went off a cliff and fell to their deaths—but they didn't. However, they did give the standard OYT description along with the very judgemental comment that he'd seen better days. Well, you try being encroached upon for 70 years while maintaining a luxurious blond mane of hair. You'd look a little worse for wear as well.

Some people think Old Yellow Top has since died. But I like to think he's gone deep into hiding because of overcrowding, bad press and misrepresentation on television. Think about what they did to the poor Bigfoot on TV in the 1970s: *Bigfoot, Aliens, The Six Million Dollar Man.* If I were Old Yellow Top, I'd run screaming as far as I could from the human race.

SMITHVILLE
(43°05'50" N, 79°32'47" W)

Smithville is a small town surrounded by farmland atop the Niagara Escarpment partway between Hamilton and Niagara Falls. It's pretty much an ordinary place as small communities go...except that it has seen a number of sightings of what can only be described as Bigfoot.

The mysterious beast in question is said to be half human and half animal. No specifics on which half is which, but I'm thinking if the top was animal and the bottom was human that would be a really weird twist. It would also raise questions about its gender (outie or innie) and whether the beast was modest enough to cover up its gender. Alas, the half-and-half description, I've learned, means not so much as half this and that half that, but a conglomeration of the two. I guess a more accurate description of the Smithville monster would have been an animal with human-like characteristics and movements.

Other words that have been used to describe the monster over the more than 10 reported sightings (and many more unreported, I suspect) include: big, furry, black, gorilla-like and evil. Evil, I tells ya! Okay, not evil. In one of the sightings that occurred closer to Campden (that's still in the general area of Smithville), oversized footprints were purportedly discovered. What else would an oversized monster leave behind but oversized footprints. I mean, if they were undersized, Smithville's monster would look like a tiptoeing ballerina as he ran away from people—and that would also probably explain why not many of these creatures have been seen. Think about it.

Anyway, as is typical with such sightings, local law enforcement has downplayed the incidents as nothing more than a series of hoaxes and sort of investigated, if squinting and saying "Well, I don't see nothin' from here" counts as investigating. I mean, why leave Tim Hortons to search for a monster in the cold, dark night when it hasn't hurt anyone and the doughnuts and coffee are free?

Cel-uh-brate Weird Times, Come On!

People meet each other in some of the oddest places. From coffeehouses to theatres, they gather and gossip, linger and laugh, yell and yak. But the weirdest of these destinations of note add a little more to the word "weird," and to the world at large, than the ordinary day-to-day goings-on of meeting and talking. They celebrate something weird, but then they also put it up in lights, sing it from the rooftops and even dress it up in lederhosen or kilts and chain mail and toast to it.

What follows are some of the weirdest destinations in Ontario, at least on a short-term basis. These are places that celebrate their weirdness for at least a short period of time each year. So, let's get inspired by Kool and the Gang and "Cel-uh-brate Weird Times, Come On!"

WIARTON WILLIE FESTIVAL
WIARTON

Wiarton is a small, more-than-pleasant town located on an inlet of Georgian Bay at the southern end of the Bruce Peninsula. It's a town of about 2300 people and was incorporated as a village in 1880. The community originally thrived on the success of its lumber industry, but it is now known for its beaches, its tourist trade and for its furry little white guy!

That's right—in this quaint little Canadian town, a strange little annual event takes place. In the dead of winter, a guy dressed to the nines and standing next to another guy in a white groundhog costume reaches into the town-sponsored den of the famous white woodchuck, Wiarton Willie, pulls

Willie from his snug-as-a-bug-in-a-rug den, hoists him high into the air and hopes the pink-eyed little albino either yawns or snores (yawning or snoring being the indications of whether winter continues or ends). I don't know, I think this annual ritual definitely falls under the "weird" heading...way weird!

In fact, I think Wiarton may be the location of the granddaddy of all weird Canadian festivals—the Wiarton Willie Festival, or as it's known to most of us in North America, Groundhog Day (February 2). Wiarton is just 240 kilometres northwest of Toronto, which puts it in a very good position for people from southern Ontario to flock there for the annual event. Ka-ching!

They've been celebrating Groundhog Day in Wiarton since 1956. Early groundhog prognosticators were named Grundoon, Sandoon and Muldoon, but were rather ordinary as groundhogs go.

Upon the arrival of the first Wiarton Willie in the 1980s, things really heated up for this weird festival. That's because the first Wiarton Willie and his successors have all been albino groundhogs. That's right—they have white fur and pink eyes and can't see too well, which is interesting considering that W.W.'s main job is to look for his shadow once a year. Oh, the strenuousness of it all! Sounds like a government job.

It may actually be a bit strenuous considering that the first Wiarton Willie died tragically just before the festival in 1999. Perhaps he knew too much and threatened to spill the beans, and the Powers That Be silenced him. Or maybe he just had no reason to live anymore. Let's face it, W.W. #1 was easily replaced that year by a stuffed, reasonable facsimile of himself. Oh, the ignominy! Since the death of the first W.W., festival organizers have kept two Wiarton Willies on hand just in case tragedy strikes again—or one gets too big for his britches!

The Wiarton Willie Festival actually runs for two weeks and includes hockey tournaments, dances, parades, snooker tournaments, a Monte Carlo night, a fish fry and a circus.

The big question? How accurate is Wiarton Willie in his predictions of a truncated winter? Well, about the same as all the various groundhog psychics. In general, groundhogs are correct less than 40 percent of the time. Neither America's Punxsutawney Phil, Manitoba's Brandon Bob, Alberta's Balzac Billy nor Nova Scotia's Shubenacadie Sam do any better. In 2006, Wiarton celebrated the 50th anniversary of its white-woodchuck-centred festival. Sadly, the current W.W. passed away in July 2006. He will be missed.

Logging Memorial

A large, bronze sculpture depicting a logging scene sits along the Trans-Canada Highway at Blind River (that's halfway between Sudbury and Sault Ste. Marie). Known as the "Northern Ontario Logging Memorial," the sculpture was created by Laura Brown Breetvelt, who calls the sculpture "The River Hogs." The scene shows two life-sized loggers trying to clear a logjam with pike poles and peaveys. Peaveys are, of course, strong poles that have moveable hooks—any logger would know that. Not being a logger but always dreaming about the possibilities, I didn't know what a peavey was, but now I do and so do you! Behind the sculpted loggers are three copper trees that stand between 5.5 and 9 metres tall. Trees, logging and loggers have been and continue to be very important in these parts, so that's why the memorial was created as part of a millennium project in the year 2000. If you're up Blind River way and viewing the memorial, I'd suggest you don't get too close—you might just get swept away when the very real looking jam clears! Apparently something like that happened to the statues of Paul Bunyan and Babe the Blue Ox that used stand outside the Timber Village Museum next door to the Logging Memorial. Or at least that's the closest I can come to the facts about their unceremonious removal... Ouch!

OKTOBERFEST
KITCHENER-WATERLOO

The twin cities of Kitchener and Waterloo are about 100 kilometres west of Toronto. The cities have always had separate governments but over the years have basically grown into one larger place. Actually, along with their other neighbour, Cambridge, they've grown into an urban area of almost 500,000 people.

Kitchener itself was originally called Berlin, but that name was changed during World War I, for obvious reasons. They didn't want to be bombed by the RAF, I guess. In fact, Kitchener celebrated its 150th birthday in 2004. That would be the physical city itself, not as either Berlin or its newest alias.

Anyway, Kitchener-Waterloo and Cambridge, as you could probably have guessed from Kitchener's original name, are known for their strong German heritage. The area is just bursting with beer and pretzels and lederhosen. And because of these strong Germanic ties and affiliations, Canada's great Bavarian festival, Oktoberfest, is held here for eight days each October... that's Oktober—*Javol*!

It's clearly a weird little festival—except that it's not little. It is only second in size to the original Oktoberfest that is held each year in Munich, Germany. And just what exactly is Oktoberfest, other than October with a "k" and "fest" on the end? It's a celebration of everything to do with beer and sausages and *gemütlichkeit. Gemütlichkeit* is German for "warm friendliness." And what else could the good people of this formerly German-named town be, but warm and friendly—and no it's not because they're drunk from the beer.

During the eight-day fest there are fashion shows, rock concerts (Rocktoberfest), demonstrations and feats by marching bands (Kapellenfest), singing contests (Oktoberfest Idol) and the granddaddy event of them all, the Thanksgiving Day Oktoberfest Parade. There's also the crowning of Miss Oktoberfest, which used to be a beauty pageant, but whose winner is now decided by a cadre of Star Chamber–like Oktoberfest officials!

The biggest and most memorable parts of the Oktoberfestin' fest really are the beer, bratwurst and schnitzel that are served up in wildly decorated halls (Festhallen) with big beer steins, sauerkraut and lots of singing and polka dancing. The whole crazy, wacky, wild fest is overseen by a happily rotund mascot named Oncle Hans, who sports a thick moustache and wears lederhosen and a felt hat. He's got a female counterpart named Tante Frieda, but for some weird reason, she's not given much attention. I guess that's the fate of mascots named Tante.

If you're looking for a family friendly, beer-swilling time, Oktoberfest runs each and every year from the Friday before Thanksgiving until the Saturday after it. And, if any Americans happen to be reading this, that's Canadian Thanksgiving.

Prost!

HAMILTON INTERNATIONAL TATTOO
HAMILTON

Hamilton is known as the "Steel City," a lunch-bucket town, even a one-way place. But did you know that it is also known as an international tattooing destination? No, it's true. I was born there, I grew up there—heck, I even go back to visit family there. But I had no idea that people came from all around the globe to take part in an international tattooing festival there. I didn't even know there was such a thing as an international tattooing festival...Wait a second. Let me do some more research!

If you have the DVD version of *Weird Ontario Places*, slow, scintillating elevator music is now playing. If not, here goes...

Nah nah nah nah nah Nuuuuh, nah nah Nuuuuh, nah nah nah nah nah Nuuuuh, nah nah Nuuuuh, nah nah nah nah nah Nuuuuh, nah nah Nuuuuh, nah nah nah nah nah Nuuuuh, nah nah Nuuuuh...

Okay, I'm back. Apparently, it's not an international tattooing festival that takes place in Hamilton each year. It actually doesn't have anything to do with tattooing at all. At least not the kind of tattooing most of us know as the inking up of one's body. But it's all predicated on a mistake in languages, so it's easy to see how I was misled.

The Hamilton event is known officially as the "Hamilton International Tattoo." But the tattoo they're talking about is pipes and drums and military bands. Say what?

Here's the official story as the HIT (Hamilton International Tattoo) conveys it. Way back in 17th-century Holland, British soldiers who were billeted there were out enjoying some pints at the local watering hole. In those days in Holland, a drummer in the streets marked and sounded the time of last call for alcohol. Instead of ye olde Dutch tavernkeep yelling "Last call!" when he heard the drum major drumming his little heart out outside, he instead yelled "*Do den taptoe*," which meant "Turn off the taps," as in taps on the beer kegs. The British soldiers, being amazing linguists, bastardized the original word *taptoe* and made it "tattoo." Tattoo doesn't at all look or sound much like *taptoe*, but then again Cartier's people thought Kanata was the name of the whole country, not just a word for the local village. So let's not get into the whole language issue here.

Anyway, eventually, over many years, the street drummer was joined by a fifer, a bugler and a piper—usually a bagpiper. This grand four-man band eventually grew larger, acquired official status and became the regimental band. As the regimental band, they played wake-up calls, taps and occasionally performed concerts for the locals. And that, my friends, is where ye olde International Tattoo came from. Aren't you glad you asked?

And the Hamilton Tattoo is no less spectacular than the convoluted tattoo explanation. The organizers assure me that you'll "thrill to the sights and sounds of the military bands, pipes and drums and some of the world's finest military and civilian performers." And that, my uniform-admiring friends, is just a hint of what you'll get at HIT.

What you're really going to experience is a bunch of marching bands (with full indoor arena–echoing sounds) and people parading around in military uniforms with their medals swinging in the wind. Actually, you can see almost the exact same things at Toronto's Gay Pride Parade. Though, I have to admit, most of the generals at Gay Pride march around in uniforms, but instead of their medals swinging in the wind it's their batons!

HIT takes place the second weekend in June at the venerable Copps Coliseum in beautiful downtown Hamilton. And if you think I won't be there, just consider this: HIT was once recognized by the American Bus Association. Then again, buses and tattoos pretty much go together, right?

BIG GARGANTUAN & RIDICULOUSLY OVERSIZED

Muskoka Chair

The "World's Largest Muskoka Chair" (or Adirondack chair, if you prefer that name) is located in Varney. This largest wooden cottage chair is 6.7 metres high and stands outside Peacock Woodcraft, a business producing cedar lawn furniture. There was some controversy over who had the biggest Muskoka chair, because the town of Gravenhurst also claimed the title. But at just under 4 metres high, clearly Gravenhurst has come up short and Varney gets the Woody. Say what? Well, as everyone knows, a "Woody" is the Muskoka chair version of an Oscar.

UFOs and Alien Sights of Hovering Interest

One of my favourite subjects is and has always been anything and everything to do with UFOs, abductions and aliens—the space kind, not the illegal, terrestrial kind. When I was a kid, I did in fact see a UFO. It is much more a fuzzy, kid-remembered image than a solid, discernable and provable fact, but such is the stuff that the UFO phenomenon is based on.

I have read—studied even—much UFO literature from books by Whitley Strieber, Budd Hopkins, Zecharia Sitchin and Canada's own John Robert Colombo to the wackiest of Internet websites. Once, I even had an e-mail correspondence with an American woman who claimed to be in contact with 12 different alien races—again we're talking interplanetary aliens, not the illegal types.

Over the years, the hype, the hardcore believers and the converted masses have all pushed me more towards

☞

scepticism than to belief. Places that are related to UFOs are elusive to a great extent because sightings happen in cities and rural areas, in every region of the province and country and rarely in the same place twice. This makes my task of pinning down a "weird" place difficult.

If you want to see UFOs, apparently they most often hang out around nuclear power facilities or military installations. With the number of military bases dwindling in Canada, it becomes far more difficult to see ET and his buddies there year after year. However, with power consumption increasing and nuclear power growing, it seems to me that those are the places to look and find the "Greys," the "Nordics" and the "Reptilians."

I have included a number of places in this section that qualify as weird and relate to UFOs: the World's First UFO Sighting Station at Shirley's Bay, the SETI telescope in Algonquin Park and the deliciously covert underground facility in North Bay called 22 Wing. However, if you're looking for a sure thing, head for the nukes and weird country will open before your very eyes.

In league with these locations, I give you a related and extrapolated possibility to do with the Sir Adam Beck Generating Station in Niagara.

☞

Ontario does not contain as many fun-filled UFO sights as Alberta with its UFO Landing Pad in St. Paul or its replica Starship Enterprise in Vulcan. However, leave it to Niagara Falls to come through in a pinch and give us "Alien Encounter"—an over-the-top museum/attraction dedicated to UFOs and aliens. It's a place that likes to make a buck and let you in on the skinny concerning aliens. Oh, and they're not afraid to talk about it...or perhaps reach out and scare the bejeezes out of you.

Let's face it, the UFO thing used to be a dirty little secret, barely talked about in serious conversation and relegated to off-colour jokes and snickers behind people's backs. But that is no more. The whole thing has developed from a niche market into a huge industry. And what better place for the industry to expand than Niagara Falls?

Ottawa and its environs really hold the key to Ontario's weird UFO places, for let's face it, there's more unidentified stuff being flung around our nation's capital than any other place in the country.

Oh, and there's one more likelihood for seeing elusive UFOs. If you live in the middle of nowhere, are out tipping cows and your name is Bob or Roy, you're bound to see one of these things. Perhaps you'll even get to appear

☞

on Canada AM *or* Breakfast Television. *But you won't be seen with Peter Mansbridge on* CBC. *The Mother Corp is much too serious a place to showcase the odd ramblings, sightings and mystic beliefs of slack-jawed gawkers. Unless you're Rex Murphy, that is!*

THE ONES THAT ARE FOR REAL

THE WORLD'S FIRST UFO SIGHTING STATION
SHIRLEY'S BAY

In the 1950s, the Canadian government was apparently not afraid to say that it was looking for UFOs. In fact, the government, under the guidance of the eminently respected Wilbert Smith and the Department of Transport, was not even afraid to say they'd set up the world's first officially sponsored Saucer Sighting Station, just 16 kilometres outside Ottawa in the community of Shirley's Bay. And at one point Smith wasn't even afraid to say that they'd sighted one. But then something happened, and the whole thing came crashing down, but not like Roswell. Let me start from the beginning.

The Saucer Sighting Station was set up by Wilbert Smith and housed in a small shack for less than a year. It wasn't manned, but it was linked by some form of alarm system to a fully manned ionospheric research station nearby. Inside the sighting station, there was equipment both expensive and complex, capable of detecting radio noise, magnetic fluctuations and gamma rays among other things.

At one point in August 1954, personnel at the station apparently detected what they thought was a flying saucer. The bells and alarms went off, and Smith and others ran outside to see what they could see. Nothing, as it turned out, because the whole area was fogged in. But this didn't stop Smith from announcing to the press that he thought he'd caught one. And that's where the glorious days of Canada's UFO sighting station go to hell in a handbasket. Soon after his announcement, Smith was reprimanded, and within the month, the Shirley's Bay project was "officially" shut down. It was an ignominious end to say the least. However, Shirley's Bay will always have the distinction of being the site of the world's first flying saucer sighting station.

THE HOLE
NORAD, NORTH BAY

"The Hole" is the affectionate name given to the underground complex that houses the tactical headquarters for Canada's contribution to NORAD (North American Aerospace Defence Command) at North Bay. One hundred eighty-three metres into the rock of the Laurentian Mountain range, a three-storey facility was built between 1959 and 1963. It's the size of two football fields, but they won't say whether that's a Canadian or American football field. The military does love its secrecy, even when it doesn't matter!

As much as 230,000 m³ of rock were removed to build the Hole. In order to gain entry to the facility, you must be strategically inserted by way of one of two tunnels—the north tunnel is 2018 metres long and the south tunnel is 1021 metres long. At the bottom of the Hole there are three entrances to the very complex complex, and each has a 18-tonne blast door that can be slammed shut should the need arise. "Should the need arise" is military code for "a nuclear blast is a-coming" or government code for "tell the civilians to duck or head for cover or any other useless thing that'll give them something to do and get them out of our way!" Or something like that.

The Hole is really Canada's penny-ante version of the American Cheyenne Mountain facility that houses the NORAD Command Center and the Air Defense Operations Center. That one is big and brash and in your face, just like some Americans—though I'm sure I never met any like that, even when I lived for two years in Washington, DC. Anyway, Canada's version of Cheyenne Mountain is talked about like it's nothing more than an underground office building. But we know better, don't we? Ahh, Canadian understatement. It's a clear and classic giveaway. And what "much bigger" thing could this clear and classic giveaway be masking? Well, space aliens, of course! Sorry, read on...

In the aforementioned Hole in North Bay, 22 Wing (that's a military base designation, not a chicken and wing franchise) provides surveillance, identification, control and warning for the air defence of Canada and North America. So, just what are they watching, controlling, warning and defending against? Well, it ain't H5N1 or Russian missiles! In fact, it's all very vague, very mysterious and very military-like (and very unconvincing, to say the least).

And this is why this facility fits into my UFO chapter. Let's face it—they're looking for UFOs in this facility, and I can prove it! A UFO is, of course, anything unidentified that is flying. That includes meteorites, missiles and well, alien craft, no? So there it is, the Hole is where 22 Wing is admittedly involved in tracking, warning and controlling UFOs. I've cracked it...or maybe I'm cracked?

And I'll go out on a limb here and say we're talking alien-type space UFOs. Why else would they talk about the blast doors like they were a "blast from the past" and be planning a move aboveground some time this year? It all fits. They're less concerned about earthly threats and more concerned about space threats, so they need to be closer to space to see the said threats.

There's one other piece of information to include about the Hole, 22 Wing and North Bay. It has been the scene of a great many—I would venture hundreds—of UFO sightings. So either there are a lot of nuts in North Bay, or North Bay is a tourist site for space visitors.

Now, officially the military and government deny this, but we all know the truth, don't we? A wink and a nod, a wink and a nod, and a wink and a nod again!

Longest Beach

The world's longest freshwater beach is 14 kilometres long and located on Georgian Bay. Most Ontarians already know that this record-breaking beach is called Wasaga Beach. It's found within Wasaga Beach Provincial Park and is divided into eight areas equipped with changing facilities, picnic tables and washrooms. Not to be outdone by its sheer size, Wasaga Beach is also incredibly beautiful!

ALGONQUIN RADIO OBSERVATORY AND SETI
ALGONQUIN PROVINCIAL PARK

The National Research Council's Algonquin Radio Observatory is located deep within Algonquin Provincial Park, well away from human interference. The observatory consists of an array of 32 parabolic reflectors, each 3 metres in diameter, a 1.8-metre dish, and a giant 46-metre dish that hovers well above the others. Looking at the stars, the sun and the planets is perhaps not that weird. However, in the 1970s and 1980s, no fewer than two teams of scientists used the Algonquin Radio Observatory to try and find extraterrestrials. Now that is a little weird and makes Algonquin Provincial Park a much more interesting and weird place. I'm not much of a wilderness kind of guy, ya see.

The scientists conducted their research on behalf of SETI. SETI is, of course, the Search for Extra-Terrestrial Intelligence. Not to be confused with the Search for Terrestrial Intelligence, though results for both have been similarly not that encouraging. (Insert rimshot here!)

Clearly, the scientists in question did not find ET or else this section would be a whole lot bigger, and who knows, maybe we'd all now be conversing telepathically instead of on paper or via the phone or Internet.

THE ONES THAT ARE STRICTLY FOR MONEY

ALIEN ENCOUNTER
NIAGARA FALLS

Lifelike, or should I say "alien-like," statues of many of your favourite movie aliens greet you as you wait in line for a truly tacky or terrifying attraction in the tacky-terrifying land known as Niagara Falls. "Alien Encounter" is a strictly entrepreneurial venture that's designed to entertain and perhaps frighten you while it frees you of some of your disposable income.

As I said, there are replica statues of movie aliens such as Yoda, ET, Predator, Jar Jar Binks and Darth Vader designed to get you in the mood and preoccupy you as you wait for the main event. You choose whether to take the family friendly Yellow Tour, during which the aliens won't touch you, or the Red Tour, where they will.

Either way, you end up in a mad inventor's type of lab, where the scientist quickly disappears and locks you in so as to make you go through the rest of the tour trying to find your way out. On the benign, family friendly side, weird noises, screams and other scare-inducing sounds accompany the rest of the tour. I don't know about the touchy-feely tour because, quite frankly, things like that scare me to death, and there was no way I was putting myself though that.

The whole thing can be kind of fun, though it's got more to do with mood lighting than anything. Admission is about $8 for kids and almost $10 for adults. If you go on the touchy-feely Red Tour, drop me a line and tell me how it went. I'm on pins and needles waiting to find out.

COLOSSUS
WOODBRIDGE

Just north of Toronto there is a multiplex movie theatre called Colossus. It has what appears to be a replica of a landed flying saucer on its roof. Colossus is big and can be seen across the flat-lands from multiple highways. Not much more to say about it than that. Except, perhaps, for the official word—lame!

THE ONE THAT'S SUBMITTED FOR YOUR CONSIDERATION

SIR ADAM BECK POWER GENERATING STATION

NIAGARA

The Sir Adam Beck Generating Station tour is run by the Niagara Parks Commission. From April through October, visitors can learn about the potential energy that is captured and generated by one of Ontario's largest hydroelectric stations. You'll discover interesting facts about this natural and reliable source of energy and what it's meant to Ontario for more than four decades. You'll learn about the power generating process and how it was developed and has evolved over time. Yadda, yadda, yadda...blah, blah, blah...bada-bing, bada-bang, bada-boom!

What you won't learn about is the great 1965 East Coast power blackout, or how the grey aliens were and/or are involved in this facility.

I know—right now, you're all saying "What?"

Well, again I've got no proof, but there has been a lot of speculation and suggestion about what caused the great blackout way back in 1965. Authorities have admitted the Adam Beck II station was at fault. However, speculation and sheer gall have put grey space aliens at the heart of this mystery.

And here's where we come to the suggestion that I make for your consideration.

What if, while someone was on the tour of the Sir Adam Beck Generating Station, he or she managed to slip away from the tour, go through a door for employees only and then manage to see what was truly going on at the "power plant"? Would that person have seen grey space aliens working hand in hand with humans to produce a new kind of power? Or perhaps something else? And how long has this been going on, what is it about and is Ontario Power Generation just an acronym for some quasi-governmental-alien hybrid body that is controlling Adam Beck and more? Well, who knows the answers to these questions and others? I mean, the wandering off from the regular tour probably never happened, nor the rest. Probably not, anyhow.

So for those of you who think I'm advocating that you should try to personalize your tour of Adam Beck, I'm not. What am I suggesting? Well, for that you'll just have to read between the lines.

THE BEST PLACES
TO SEE UFOS

As I said in the intro to this chapter, nuclear power plants are clearly the frontrunners in terms of places where you're most likely to see UFOs. But did you know that there are a great many nuclear reactors throughout the province that are used "officially" for research purposes? Here's a list of locations known to have had or currently have nuclear reactors. Hover near them, and you're bound to see ET.

The actual power producing facilities are: the Darlington Generating Station in Bowmanville; the Pickering Generating Station in Pickering; and the Bruce Generating Station in Tiverton.

Research reactors exist at: Chalk River, Kanata (Ottawa), Tunney's Pasture (Ottawa), McMaster University (Hamilton), Royal Military College (Kingston) and the University of Toronto (currently shut down).

Naturally
Nutty Nature

A magnetic hill, white, black and red squirrels, a sleeping giant, a big head, the Grand Canyon of Ontario, the largest freshwater island in the world and water, water everywhere. It's all the weirdest naturally occurring flora, fauna and water that Mother Nature has to throw at Ontario. Take your pick. Whichever you choose, the naturally nutty nature of nature is, well...unnatural, naturally speaking.

Does that make any sense? Not really, but nothing outdoes the nutty nature of nature. It confounds, discombobulates and defies explanation—except by scientists, psychics and parapsychologists—provides tourist attractions, and gives a bit of mystery to some places that might otherwise seem ordinary. And none of these Ontario gems is ordinary. They may be understated and avoid traditional hype, but that's the nature of natural places categorized as weird. And these Ontario places are naturally weird, naturally!

MAGNETIC HILL
BURLINGTON

The magnetic hill in Burlington is starting to rival the one in Moncton, New Brunswick, for fame. And that is mainly because a cheesy television show perpetuates mysterious folkloric tales involving the hill, many car accidents and the ghosts of children who died in a bus crash.

However, Burlington's Magnetic Hill is no more a mystery, magnetic or ghostly, than any of the others. It is an optical illusion, pure and simple. I should know—I grew up in Hamilton, a stone's throw from Burlington's Magnetic Hill. I've been there many times and never felt anything creepy, dead-kid related or ghostly about it—though a friend and I once ran over a groundhog (by accident) on that road on his motorcycle and I understand there's recent word of a groundhog ghost that also frequents the locale. Actually, the groundhog ghost isn't true, and as far as I can tell, there are no records of the purported kid-killing bus crash either. However, facts have never kept TV shows like *Creepy Canada* nor TV channels like CTV Travel from popularizing and publicizing the myth.

It has also been suggested that UFOs are somehow related to the phenomenon. Because, of course, aliens would get great pleasure from taking a jaunt over to Burlington and messing with the inhabitants' minds in the form of pulling their rather primitive vehicles backwards up a hill! I wonder what message they're trying to send to us? Perhaps it's "Boo!" or "You are such dumb beings that we just can't believe it!"

If you want to visit the Burlington Magnetic Hill, it's north of Highway 403 on a rural part of King Road. You'll want to stop your car at the Hydro right-of-way entrance to begin your ride. Make your way past the UFOs lined up on the right and the buses of full of ghost kids on the left. And watch out for the groundhogs, whatever you do!

THE WHITE SQUIRRELS
EXETER

So, do white squirrels actually exist or is this some twisted marketing campaign in which the tree rats with the furry tails are spray painted as a come-on?

Well, actually they do exist—no paint, no come-on and no pink eyes. And that is one of the most unique things about Exeter's white squirrel population. Whereas other towns in North America promote their white albino squirrels—pink eyes and all—Exeter's white squirrels aren't albino. They are regular squirrels that just happen to be white. Think "Man from Glad," but in squirrel form.

And in Exeter, the townsfolk and visitors celebrate these unique tree-dwelling rodents with the annual White Squirrel Festival each September. There's a parade and various white squirrel events attended by white squirrel mascots galore—and townsfolk and visitors as well. The official mascot is named "White Wonder." Wonder why? Well, he's wonderfully white, of course!

The origin of Exeter's white squirrels is unclear, though it's been suggested the following groups had something to do with it: Gypsies, tropical visitors and even Torontonians. If you visit Exeter other than at festival time, the white squirrels can be seen all over town and especially in MacNaughton Park. Exeter is located 50 kilometres north of London, Ontario.

THE BLACK SQUIRRELS
LONDON

Not to be outdone by the Exeter mighty whites, London boasts a population of black squirrels in Victoria Park. No festival— yet—but these black devils were actually exported to the campus of Ohio's Kent State University in the early 1960s. And then came the Kent State massacre. I'm not exactly sure what else makes these black squirrels unique, odd or weird. I get the white squirrel oddity—unusual, right? And a white squirrel definitely stands out in a crowd. The black ones, not so much! Unless they're in a crowd of white squirrels, that is. But hey, but what do I know?

BIG
GARGANTUAN &
RIDICULOUSLY
OVERSIZED

Sundial Folly

Sundial Folly is located at the foot of York Street in Harbour Square Park West in Toronto. People call it "that cracked egg thing," the "concrete ball" or "that round thing over there." The folly has a ramp leading into a hollow concrete sphere 6.7 metres in diameter with a piece about a metre in diameter removed on the harbour side. This cutout allows sunlight into the sphere and frames a view of the inner harbour and the Toronto Islands. There is also a cascading wall of water beside the orb and a circulating pool beside and inside it. The whole thing kind of looks like Mork from Ork just landed and his egg ship is sinking into the harbour because he forgot to shut the door. No, really. Picture it. Sundial Folly was unveiled in 1995 and was the first project by two talented architecture grads fresh out of the University of Waterloo. Their winning design beat out 144 other proposals, some of them by very well-known and established artists. I bet that's got to hurt! The unique sculpture has been used for many things, including a homeless shelter, teenage drinking place and, my absolute favourite, the stage for a 1999 performance piece featuring a dancer, a mezzo-soprano and musicians playing clarinet and hurdy-gurdy. Folly indeed!

MANITOULIN ISLAND

So, what does being the largest island in a freshwater lake in the world get you besides being a question on every quiz show ever broadcast on TV? Well, there are the tourists who tramp all over your beautiful wilderness and, well, the laurels. Let's not forget the laurels, because you are the "Largest Island in a Freshwater Lake" in the whole entire world. That's 2766 km^2 of island, don't ya know. Have I mentioned it's within a freshwater lake?

What is also interesting—or weird—is that there are also 110 inland lakes on Manitoulin Island. Within many of those lakes you've also got many islands. Say what? Well here goes: Treasure Island is in Mindemoya Lake; Mindemoya Lake is on Manitoulin Island; Manitoulin Island is in Georgian Bay; Georgian Bay is in Lake Huron; Lake Huron is in North America; North America is on Earth. That's pretty cool, eh?

Manitoulin Island—it's big and freshly watered and weird. No, really!

SLEEPING GIANT ISLAND
LAKE SUPERIOR

Looking out across Lake Superior from Thunder Bay, you can distinctly see the form of a giant in the water with his arms folded across his beefy chest... Or that's what they say, anyway. I've kind of seen it by squinting and unfocusing my eyes like I'm looking at a "Magic Eye" piece of art. The phenomenon is not (surprise, surprise) a real sleeping giant. It's the formation of flora and fauna on an island.

However, First Nations tradition says the Sleeping Giant is none other than the Great Spirit, Nanabijou. The rather long and somewhat complicated legend basically says that Nanabijou

awarded a loyal Ojibwa tribe access to a great silver mine, with the stipulation that they keep the location a secret from the white men or else both the Ojibwa and Nanabijou would suffer the consequences. Sioux rivals coveted the silver, so a seasoned Sioux scout infiltrated the Ojibwa tribe, learned the mine's location and then inadvertently told it to some white men after they got him drunk. The result was as warned: Nanabijou was turned to stone and became the Sleeping Giant in the water and the Ojibwa disappeared.

It's hard to say who's to blame here—Nanabijou for his poor judgement in showing off the wealth; the Ojibwa for not doing enough to protect the secret mine; the covetous Sioux who couldn't hold their liquor; or the evil white men. In the end, life's too short, grudges are pointless and Sleeping Giant Island is rather picturesque.

OUIMET CANYON AND THE BIG INDIAN HEAD

Ouimet Canyon has been compared to the much more famous Grand Canyon. Which, of course, means it pales in comparison to the original...un-huh!

However, Ouimet Canyon does have some things of note to, ah, note! It's 100 metres deep, 150 metres wide and 2 kilometres long. Okay, those aren't the real notable things about this gorgeous gorge, but they do set a three-dimensional scene. More notable are the sheer-walled canyon, the boulder-laden floor and the rare arctic alpine plants that grow on the valley floor. Now it's sounding a bit more like the Grand Canyon, *non*? The canyon's unusual flora includes subarctic thickets, fir-club moss and encrusted saxifrage. Wowee! I mean how often does one encounter encrusted saxifrage unless you're in the middle of a celebrity scrum at the Toronto International Film Festival...or in the subarctic...or something.

Anyway, for those who wish to know, the canyon's rocks were formed by horizontally flowing magma that flowed under the earth's surface and created a sill—like at your front door or at the bottom of your window. All that happened, oh, a billion or so years ago. Let's just say it was long before Medicare came to Canada, so magma burn victims had to fend for themselves at the time. Later, glaciers swept across the area, broke the sill and when they retreated, left broken rock that was eventually carved into the canyon by water, rain, erosion and stuff like that. That's the scientific explanation.

The legend handed down from First Nation's peoples is much more colourful, full of intrigue, murder, love and over-the-top drama. You know, the way a legend should be.

As it goes, a long time ago, there was a giant named Omett who was helping Nanabijou carve out the lakes and make the mountains. I guess they're kind of forerunners to Paul Bunyan and Babe the Blue Ox. Omett was, of course, in love with Nanabijou's daughter, Naiomi. Legend doesn't say what Naiomi's claim to fame was other than being convenient tragic daughter material. Anyway, one day when Omett was moving a mountain, the clumsy oaf dropped part of it on Naiomi and killed her. He freaked out, buried her and said "Hey, haven't seen her" when a panicked Nanabijou came looking. But old Nanabijou sensed something lay underground, so he flung a lightning bolt, which split open the earth, created the canyon and revealed the body of his dead daughter. Nanabijou then put two and two together, turned Omett to stone and put him on the canyon wall to watch over his daughter's grave forever.

And now a visit to Ouimet Canyon isn't complete without seeing the big ugly rock column known as the Indian Head. And before I get nasty letters, "Indian Head" is the official name, not my own personal politically incorrect term.

Ouimet Canyon and its funky Indian Head are a short drive northwest of Thunder Bay. You can view the canyon and all its fun, cool and weird flora and fauna via two viewing platforms that extend out beyond the spectacular sheer cliffs, though the fragility of the ecosystem does not allow you to visit the canyon floor itself. And if you're ever moving a mountain, tell your boss's daughter to get out of the way before you do so or you too might end up as a big, ugly head!

FATHOM FIVE NATIONAL MARINE PARK
GEORGIAN BAY

A whole submerged world of wonder awaits you, if you dare dive at Fathom Five. Mwah, ah, ahhhh! So says the press material. Or at least it would if a reincarnated P.T. Barnum or a TV promo person got hold of it. You know, a person that could really only be described as—LIAR!

In any event, Fathom Five is, in fact, Canada's first National Marine Conservation Area. I also have to say that Fathom Five is a very cool name and absolutely unlike anything bureaucrats usually come up with for these types of places.

Located at the mouth of Georgian Bay, the park contains a whole lot to see for the underwater scuba enthusiast. For me, not so much. But that's only because the whole idea of artificially breathing air through a hose while underwater gives me the heebee-geebies. And the hooby-goobies and yukky-wukkies! Swimming I don't mind, but underwater breathing, no thanks.

However, that does not discount the weird underwater world that Fathom Five presents. There are at least 22 shipwrecks, a submerged former waterfall that once would have rivalled or outdone Niagara, and ancient underwater trees that date back 7500 years. Just let Disney try to top that.

The whole place is literally swimming with scientists doing research along with the private scuba diving guys and girls. But don't let that stop you. And if you're like me and not into the underwater breathing apparatuses, there's also a bunch of islands with snakes, bears and historic lighthouses to explore on foot. Flowerpot Island (now that sounds nice, doesn't it?) is the only island within Fathom Five that has trails, washrooms, picnic shelters and camping. It also has cute little red squirrels who'll use their cuteness as a ruse and steal your lunch. So beware of Yogi in his tiny red-and-fuzzy-tailed disguise. He might just get your pic-i-nic basket!

THE HORSESHOE FALLS
NIAGARA FALLS

What can you say about Niagara Falls except maybe, wow...or wowee...or wowee-wow-wow! Of course, when I'm talking about Niagara Falls, I'm actually talking about the Horseshoe Falls or Canadian Falls, not the smaller and less spectacular American Falls. And I'm also not talking about the weird and wacky town that's grown up on the Canadian side! Though if you look else-where in this book, you'll find it here too.

"The Falls," as they're known to locals, fall 52 metres, and the horseshoe has a length at its brink of 792 metres from Goat Island to Table Rock! Every minute, 168,000 m^3 of water cascade over the Falls. However none of these statistics even comes close to making any sort of record. There are other falls that are

taller, wider and have more water volume than Niagara, however, there are few, if any, that are visited by tourists as often—
some 12 million people per year. And standing there looking
at the Falls, whether it's from next to the brink or underneath at
the Journey Behind the Falls or from the deck of the Maid of the
Mist, it is nothing if not spec-tac-u-lar!

At night, the Falls are lit up like a Christmas tree, and in winter,
they can be even more fantastic with their oddly shaped out-
croppings of ice. The Falls don't actually freeze over in winter,
however, the falling water and mist create ice formations that, if
the winter is long and cold enough, actually form an ice bridge
across the river.

But that's not what makes the Falls weird, either. The fact that
you can safely get close enough to the Falls to actually feel their
thunder is pretty wild as well. What really makes the Falls weird
is that for hundreds of years, they've drawn adventurers who
think the Falls can be tamed. That's right, what makes the Falls
so weird is that people, despite the more than obvious dangers,
keep trying to tame the Falls. And by tame the Falls, I mean
these people try to conquer the raging waters by diving in and

going over the brink with the hope of continuing to live. And some actually do survive.

The first recorded person to go over Niagara Falls in a barrel and live was a woman named Annie Taylor, who did so in 1901. There have been numerous other attempts and variations on the barrel theme over the years. People have used steel barrels, rubber balls and barrels wrapped in inner tubes for their Falls trips. Others have gone over the brink with nothing but what God gave them—absolutely no common sense. There's even one unfortunate gentleman who attempted to ride a jet ski over the falls and parachute to the bottom to raise awareness for homeless issues. Unfortunately, he raised a lot more awareness about parachute safety when his did not open.

If you wish to learn more about the "daredevils," you can visit the Daredevil Museum at 303 Rainbow Boulevard at 3rd Street. It's free. However, much more spectacular is to go to Table Rock and just look over the brink at the spectacular Falls. Who knows—you may be there on a day that a daredevil arrives in full daredevil mode. You probably want to hope not, though.

Streets of Distraction

As weird places go, streets may seem, at least on the surface, an "outside" destination. How's that for a little play on words? But don't forget, there are a great many streets in the world that one could easily classify as weird: Lombard Street in San Francisco twists and turns; Fremont Street in Las Vegas is covered by a flashy, tacky light display; and the Grand Canal in Venice is, well, all wet!

So, here are Ontario's weirdest streets!

YONGE STREET
TORONTO TO...

The longest street in the world is located, well, in most of Ontario. That's right—at 1896 kilometres, the longest street in the world starts out at Lake Ontario in Toronto as Yonge Street and winds its way around to the Minnesota border at Rainy River as Highway 11. Clearly it's not a straight path, and the name Yonge Street changes to Highway 11 just north of Barrie. Upper Canada's governor, John Graves Simcoe, named Yonge Street in 1796 for Sir George Yonge, who was Britain's Secretary of War at the time. Because of the street's twists and turns and the name changes, some people dispute Yonge Street's "Longest Street in the World" status. But let's face it—they're all just jealous quibblers!

CHURCH STREET
(BETWEEN BLOOR AND GERRARD)
TORONTO

It's a man! It's a woman! Actually, it's kind of both. And that, my friends, is not an unusual utterance heard on Toronto's Church Street. This, I will admit, tends to put Church Street squarely in the category of weird, and for those of us who live here, we don't mind that at all.

Church Street, and more specifically the crossroads of Church and Wellesley, is ground zero for Toronto's Gay Community. The Gaybourhood, as some of us like to call it, is lively, crowded, downtown, and as I alluded to earlier, my home. The G-hood, roughly bounded by Bloor, Jarvis, Gerrard and Yonge Streets, makes up Canada's largest gay village. Some people call it the ghetto, but I think not. And since at least 80 percent of people define themselves as not gay, lesbian or transgendered, the G-hood is probably pretty weird for most.

Within the G-hood, there are bars, restaurants, nightclubs, bath-houses and even regular-type establishments such as banks, dry cleaners and a hardware store. Who knew the "gays" did regular stuff like others, right Martha? There are also plenty of places to live, a beer store and even a gay statue. Oh, make it go away, Martha. That's too much gay!

But anyway, let me tell you the story about the gay statue. The 4.1-metre-tall bronze and granite monument depicts Alexander Wood, who stands 2.5 metres tall and cuts quite a dapper figure in his long coat, top hat and more than obvious bulging place. History tells us that Wood was a 19th-century magistrate in the old city of York—that's what Toronto used to be called. He became famous in 1810 for being run out of town under a cloud of homosexual scandal. That came after Wood delved too deeply when investigating a rape case. The female victim claimed to have scratched the genitals of her attacker, so Wood took it upon himself to examine the accused's nether regions. Rumours spread, the story exploded, and Wood soon departed for his native Scotland. Apparently, leering at another man's genitals was not a crime in Scotland. Guess it can't be helped in a land where the lads wear kilts.

After being exiled for a few years, Wood returned to York and bought up the land where the Gaybourhood is now located. It became known as Molly Wood's Bush—"molly" being a derogatory term for homosexual that dates back to the 1810s.

In any event, a visit to the modern Molly Wood's Bush will certainly set your tongue a-waggin' and your mouth a-gapin'...or other things, depending on who you are and what you're doing here. There are men holding hands with men, women holding hands with women, and boys and girls dressed up as girls and boys respectively. On Pride Weekend (in late June) and during Folsom Fair North (mid-July), you're more likely to see exposed skin and even genitalia of all shapes and sizes. Molly Wood would be proud! At Halloween, there's absolutely no telling what you'll see except that it will be wild, stylish and outrageous! So, come see.

BIG

GARGANTUAN &
RIDICULOUSLY
OVERSIZED

Botanical Gardens

Burlington's Royal Botanical Gardens (RBG) is home to the world's largest collection of lilacs...sort of. Well, normally the record is accurate and stands pat, however tragedy has struck the lilac collection at the RBG. Dum dum dummmm! That's right—the lilac collection has suffered the effects of a bacterium, and now according to Harry Jongerden, a designer/horticulturalist with the RBG, it can only safely be said that the RBG has *one* of the largest collections of lilacs in the world. Is this a simple case of a bacterium innocently finding its way into the beautiful Royal Botanical Gardens? Or have some rival and jealous horticulturalists perpetrated some corporate espionage/germ warfare on the RBG? Probably just the former, but will we ever know for sure? It may be a conspiracy of the highest order...or not...

Hey, let's face it, with the RBG being located so close to Hamilton's steel mills, we should probably be grateful that all they've suffered is a bacterium infestation and not giant mutant plants devouring people. Kidding...because I mean, that's not possible...

There are a few other things about the Royal Botanical Gardens that you may want to mull over, though. In its 1100 hectares, it has one fifth of the total plant diversity in Canada; the area comprises a unique microclimate; and the lilac collection includes 400 taxa (that's species and cultivars). In addition to its spectacular and diverse collection of lilacs, the RBG also has one of the largest iris collections in the world, which comprise more than 900 taxa. So the RBG and its on-again off-again record is nothing to sneeze at...unless you have plant allergies, that is.

And here's one final thought—the RBG's Lilac Dell is the envy of the world, so if we can't defeat al-Qaeda with arms, why not try lilacs?

SPADINA AVENUE (FROM BLOOR STREET TO FRONT STREET)
TORONTO

Toronto's Spadina Avenue (from Front Street to Bloor Street) is unusual, not because it cuts through the heart of three of Toronto's historic areas (Chinatown, the University of Toronto and the Fashion District), but because the city and the TTC (Toronto Transit Commission) commissioned an odd bunch of kitschy "art" objects to be displayed along the Spadina streetcar line. The idea was not to cover up blight, but to enhance the transit-riding experience. And just what could enhance a ride on the famous Red Rocket streetcars? Free rides? No, no, no! The answer is—22 pieces of public art intended to express "the rich history and diverse cultural heritage of Toronto," or so says the brochure for the "Art On Spadina" project. The art includes an art parkette ("parkette" is a Toronto word for a really small park that often doesn't contain enough green space for a dog to poop on), a bunch of art objects atop poles raised 6 metres into the air on the transit median and community markers screaming Chinatown, University of Toronto and Fashion District. All of the art objects also have some relation to their position along the street. It's big street art that keeps on giving.

To get the full experience of Art On Spadina, you'll actually want to forego the streetcar and take a walk. It'll be quite a good workout though, since it's about 3 kilometres from Bloor Street to Front Street, but hey, it's Art On Spadina!

At Bloor Street, there is a parkette with a large set of black granite dominos, big enough to sit on, but unfortunately, not movable enough to play with. At Sussex Street, atop two 6-metre-high poles are bronze castings of a Sussex rooster and a Sussex spaniel. The animals originated in (you guessed it!) Sussex in southern England, and this Toronto street was probably named after the same county, though there is no definitive proof of that.

On to Harbord Street, where the highflying pole colonnade continues with interpretive sculptures depicting images taken from the coat of arms of the University of Toronto (beaver, book, tree and crown). Harbord Street, for those not in the know, is where you'll find one of the entrances to the University of Toronto. And thank goodness there is a book in among those images, or people would start to wonder what is actually being taught at the U of T.

At Willcocks Street, there's a sundial and a milk bottle. The sundial is in reference to an ornamental garden that once stood at Knox College Circle (which Spadina wraps around at this point), and the bottle refers the city's first dairy, the City Dairy Company. There's also a subtextual Latin reference to the production of penicillin at Knox College and a painter's brush. It's all a bit obscure, but it's public art. Public art fun!

At College Street, you'll find "Fowl Play," that being the name of the pole-top art pieces—an aluminum rooster and hen—found there, not a mugging in progress. If you're lucky, that is. Just kidding! Well, sort of kidding.

At the entrance to Kensington Market, you'll see a globe at Baldwin Street that's circled by images taken from the wares sold in Kensington Market: clothing, meat, vegetables and odorous fish and cheese. At St. Andrews Street, there's a cat on a kitchen chair. If you take a slight detour and walk through Kensington Market, you'll realize that the cat sculpture is particularly appropriate for this community's marker, for cats with attitude Kensington has aplenty!

The entrance to Chinatown is at Dundas Street and the community marker here incorporates images from Chinese mythology, including a phoenix, dragon, monkey and unicorn. There's another dragon, though displayed differently, at Sullivan Street. He pokes his head through a window frame on the pole on the east side of the transit median. On the west side of the median, there's another window that contains a cornucopia underneath a ripening grape arbour that's supposed to represent "the energy of the harvest and the Mediterranean and European traditions fulfilled in the New World." Blood, sweat and no head tax, oh my!

At Queen Street, you'll see the start of a section of street theatre depicting social and ethnic scenes from Spadina's past. The pieces of pole art here and at King and Front Streets are supposed to look like the original hydro poles that were found on Spadina. You know, wooden poles with crosshatched, antenna-like tops. Homage to hydro pole—what a concept! The Queen Street north pole features a silhouette of "Dancers, Film Crew and the World" and "Lion Dance"; the south pole has musicians, a shopkeeper, and the "Bargain Benny's Pickfair Turret." If the art at Queen Street all sounds a little much to take in, don't despair. I'd suggest you take it in quickly and head around the corner to one of the local watering holes and have a restive (or reflective) pint!

And after the pint, you can continue on to Richmond Street and the monument to the Fashion District, which was the main industry along Spadina for much of the 20th century. This community marker has a 1.2-metre-high pile of very large and colourful concrete buttons capped by a 1.7-metre-tall bronze thimble. No accompanying oversized needle, though. I guess the city thought someone might poke out an eye...or a pancreas?

At King Street, there are two hydro-pole-type markers with silhouette images that include a May Day march, presser, model, sewing machines, fur worker's strike and a dressmaker's form.

The final bit of street theatre is found at Front Street, where more hydro-pole-inspired silhouettes feature immigrants, Emancipation Day 1961, a newsboy, a streetcar and a horse and buggy.

Depending on how many pints you've had, you'll either love Art On Spadina or not finish the whole tour. Either way, the streetcar's just steps away.

DOWNTOWN STREETS
HAMILTON

This time I'm not talking about just one weird street or even intersecting weird streets—this time I'm talking about all the streets in downtown Hamilton. And just why...and how...and what the heck? "They're all one way!" That's often what you hear from people who don't live in Hamilton, haven't lived there long or are what my mother and some other Hamiltonians call "Toronto people."

I actually fall into the category of "Toronto people" in my mother's eyes, since I haven't lived in the city of my birth for more than 20 years. However, in terms of the weird one-way street issue, I'm actually with my mother on this one.

The weirdness perpetrated on Hamilton by outsiders is that all the streets in Hamilton are one way. Well, actually they aren't. However, a good number of downtown streets are, in fact, one-way. And there is a very good explanation for this. Traffic flow! That's right, the streets of Hamilton flow better than those of any other berg of its size I've visited, largely because the enlightened city governments of years gone by made alternating streets into one way streets running in opposite directions.

By doing that, parallel streets such as Main and King became four-lane thoroughfares in one direction, separated by a whole city block. Can you imagine what that does to traffic flow at rush hour? Well, in Hamilton, on those streets in rush hours,

the traffic does in fact rush! Main and King Streets have been great crosstown timesavers for years. James and John Streets were also paired and ran in opposite directions north and south, to the bay or to the mountain. They worked great, even if they were a bit weird to the uninitiated outsider.

But now a chink in the armour of Hamilton's weird streets has appeared. Just recently, James and John Streets south, along with St. Joseph and Charlton Streets were returned from one-way land and became two-way streets again. The idea behind the move was to try and to keep people from using these streets as simply driving roads and get drivers to stop in and spend their money at businesses along the way. My mother blames a former radio-personality-turned-politician named Bob Bratina. In fact, Bratina is probably taking most of the flak and some of the accolades for the move, but he wasn't even on city council when the decision was made. However, he is unapologetic in his support of the street direction change.

The verdict is still out on the success of this change. Although to my mother and many others, the street direction change and the cost of it are absolutely "stupid." Opinions are usually clearly expressed in my hometown, and I don't often do this, but in this instance, I have to agree with my mother. Common sense says the plan supported by Bratina is at best foolhardy. Bratina explained his ideas in a letter to a constituent, which was provided to me: "We're trying to stop the developers from spreading farther out into the countryside, we're building new condominiums and other residences in the downtown area, and we're turning the streets back to servicing the residents, businesses and shoppers downtown."

In essence, Bratina and his ilk say they are trying to get Hamilton's downtown core to thrive again. They want it to become a vibrant area where people live, work and shop. This is all a very good thing. However, he is also trying to get people from other parts of the city to come to his ward and spend their cash. History has proven again and again that this will not happen. He's trying to turn back the reign of the automobile and the sprawl perpetrated by developers. However, the genie was let out of the bottle long ago and putting it back in is going to take more than changing the driving directions on a couple of streets. They've been trying to achieve this end for as along as I have been alive. It's never worked.

So, Bob Bratina, I think you need to let it go and instead focus on creating a vibrant community in your ward—a place where people work, live and shop. And let people in other parts of the city pass through as quickly or as slowly as they wish.

Let's also not forget to focus on the positive things that outsiders say about Hamilton. "It's weird because all the streets are one way." That's a lot better than what people used to say: "Hamilton stinks!"

BIG
GARGANTUAN &
RIDICULOUSLY
OVERSIZED

North Bay

Okay, I think the kindest thing I can say about this North Bay monument is that it's large...and, well...has a presence? Some of the worst things I have heard about this monument are things like: "What kind of a First Nation's head phallus is that?"...except that the descriptions use other, more graphically descriptive words than "First Nation's" or "phallus" to describe the monument. Such is the fun of the 7.6-metre-tall, huge pine carving of a Native American replete with a couple of tall, carved feathers. It's called "Nibiising," which in Ojibwa apparently means "Beside the Large Lake." The sculptor—a man named Peter "Wolf" Toth—emigrated from Hungary to the United States in 1956 and had a personal mission to complete one of these sculptures "memorializing the first people of the land" in every U.S. state. Having achieved his goal in the late 1980s, Toth turned his attention to Canada and Mexico. Oh, why won't people just leave us alone? I mean, great! He created another such sculpture at Winnipeg Beach in Manitoba, but North Bay was the first Canadian monument in his "Trail of the Whispering Giants" series. And that, my friends, is why there is a giant cigar-shaped, and dare I say, stylized head of apparent "First Nation's origin" in North Bay. By the way, there is no giant cigar store nearby! Smoke 'em if you've got'em!

You've Got
To Be Kidding!

If you want to see some weird little gems,
Ontario's got a lot more than phlegm!
(A Tourism Ontario promotional idea)

This may not be a good idea, but it does rhyme. And
who doesn't like a rhyme? And a rhyme using the word
"phlegm"? Now that is unique—and truly weird! I mean
the word itself is weird. It conjures up a whole lot of yuck.
And so do the places in this chapter, which mostly people
will just shake their heads about and ask why, or just simply
say "you've got to be kidding!"

And yet, no one's kidding. In this one you get a mixed bag
of, well, stuff: a research-related place that's so weird they
had to put it under Sudbury; museums that only government
grants and huge closets could create; a water park with a
hairy scary twist; and one place that proves there's always
someone somewhere who'll display just about any old crap
and smile and be proud of it—or sing!

You have to admire people's unbelievable guile. So, enjoy all
the phlegm this chapter has to offer and know it's okay to
shake your head and say "You've got to be kidding!"

BATA SHOE MUSEUM
TORONTO

Every foot of space inside Toronto's Bata Shoe Museum is dedicated to the history of footwear! It was set up by the Bata family in 1991, and much of its collection was donated by Mrs. Sonja Bata, the co-founder of Bata Shoes. I guess she's the Toronto counterpart to Imelda Marcos, but without the dictatorial husband...I assume. The museum building was designed by Raymond Moriyama and is supposed to look like a shoebox that is being opened— and it kind of docs.

CANADIAN CANOE MUSEUM
PETERBOROUGH

North America's only museum dedicated to the canoe is located in Peterborough. I'm not sure whether I should applaud, laugh or cry. That's right, the Canadian Canoe Museum is real. It's no joke! The museum has more than 600 canoes and kayaks from across Canada and watercraft from around the world. It also has more than 1000 related artifacts. I guess there's more than one way to say "paddle." The museum's Weston National Heritage Centre contains nine feature exhibits: The Grand Portage, Origins Gallery, Trade and Alliance, Preserving Skills Gallery, The Land Becomes Canada, It Wasn't All Work, Summer Strokes, The Peterborough Tradition, and Reflections: The Land, the People and the Canoe. The museum has foisted itself upon Peterborough—that is, it is located in Peterborough because from 1850 to 1960, Peterborough was the world's foremost canoe-building centre. And you thought it was just cottages and lakes!

THE SHANIA TWAIN CENTRE
TIMMINS

Timmins is the hometown of both Shania Twain and the museum dedicated in her honour. The Shania Twain Centre is located on-site at the Timmins Underground Mine Tour. And if you think this is some chintzy little cardboard display with bebopping music you'll never get out of your head unless you drive a spike through it—you're half right. They've spent $11 million creating this interactive showcase dedicated to Shania's life, starting with her humble beginnings and following her achievements through to international stardom. But does fame, fortune, international stardom or a museum to her greatness answer the question of whether or not she's any good? It's a matter of taste, I guess. Much of what you'll see at the Centre is memorabilia donated by Shania herself. The Centre estimates that its display will bring an additional 55,000 visitors to Timmins each year who will spend more than $7.2 million. With those stats, I guess Shania is like the Moses of northern Ontario, but without the long, grey beard…at least as far as I know.

POLAR BEAR HABITAT
COCHRANE

Have you ever thought about how much fun it would be to swim with polar bears? Up until the time they rip your head off and suck your stomach out through your gaping neck wound, that is. Well, the good and smart people at the Cochrane Polar Bear Habitat have figured out a way for you to take that swim without the gruesome consequences. And you don't have to dress up as a lady polar bear, either, which is good, because that could lead to some other embarrassing consequences. At this unique facility, they've built a wading pool beside the actual polar bear pool. Adults and kids alike can wade in and appear to swim with the crafty white behemoths. The truth is that a thick pane of glass safely separates the two species. So, you can get in there and swim or even taunt the bears with balls and noisemakers or even herring. You could also try and find out just how much herring taunting it takes to get a polar bear mad enough to find a way through the protective glass. Oh, what Polar Bear Habitat fun!

MILDRED M. MAHONEY DOLLS HOUSE GALLERY
FORT ERIE

Just what could be the most appropriate things to display in a former Fort Erie home that served as a safe house for escaping American slaves before the U.S. Civil War? Dollhouses, of course. That's right, that's what they've done at Bertie Hall, which is located at 657 Niagara Blvd. in Fort Erie and was, in fact, a stop on the infamous Underground Railroad. The Mildred M. Mahoney Dolls House Gallery is a collection of 140 dollhouses and miniatures, which date from 1780 to 1990. All the dollhouses and miniatures on display originated in England, Germany, France, the United States and Canada. And as a sign of respect, all the American dollhouses come with miniature trapdoors and slaves hiding inside. Just kidding.

SCIENCE NORTH
SUDBURY

So, just which famous Ontario museum was built in the shape of two snowflakes? That's right, it's Sudbury's Science North. Which is a bit odd when you think about it, because apparently no two snowflakes are alike. The snowflakian science spot opened in 1984 on the shores of Lake Ramsey and remains northern Ontario's most popular tourist attraction. Oh, and by the way, a rock tunnel connects the two snowflake-shaped buildings. That is also a bit odd because snowflakes are rarely connected by rock tunnels, except in James Bond movies. But let's not forget that Science North is a Moriyama. Raymond Moriyama, that is. He's the famous Canadian architect who designed the flaky science teaching structure. By the way, the entry password is $E=mc^2$. But don't tell anyone.

BIG
GARGANTUAN &
RIDICULOUSLY
OVERSIZED

Wildlife Mural

What may be the "World's Largest Wildlife Murals" can be seen on three sides of the Canyon County Service Station (and gift shop) in Dorion. Dorion, for those who aren't as geographically knowledgeable as I am, is 70 kilometres east of Thunder Bay and lies on the north shore of Lake Superior. An artist of some note named Michael O'Connor was commissioned to paint the murals on the building in the year 2000. The east wall displays a very large (7.3 metres by 21.3 metres) and detailed moose with his antlers held high. The west wall depicts a pack of wolves—the real ones, not the lowly journal-writing kind. The mural on the south wall is the largest and covers a whopping 465 m². It is called "Dorion Memories" and depicts various things that Dorion is famous for. Heck, I didn't know Dorion was famous for anything. But I digress. The mural shows three large photographs on a background of faux wood. The world record brook trout jumps out of the centre photograph attached to the actual lure that caught him. In the year 2000, the mural won the "I Painted Some Really Big Stuff on the Side of a Gas Station and Now I Don't Know What to do With It Competition." Ahem...Actually, it won first place over hundreds of other murals created worldwide in the Airbrush Action International Mural Competition. What else would you expect on the shores of a lake named Superior than really big pictures and a really big win?

SOLAR NEUTRINO OBSERVATORY
SUDBURY

An active nickel mine 2 kilometres below the earth's surface near Sudbury is the site of a Solar Neutrino Observatory. Neutrinos are tiny particles of matter produced by fusion reactions in the sun. They are extremely difficult to detect and are probably most famous because they were talked about and used by Data and Geordi La Forge on *Star Trek: The Next Generation*. The Sudbury Observatory is unique in that it uses 1000 tonnes of heavy water to trap different kinds of neutrino interactions. Which is heav-y, man, considering that heavy water (D_2O) is 10 percent heavier than regular water (H_2O) because heavy water has two deuterium (D) atoms, which each have a nucleus containing a single proton and no neutrons. If this makes sense to you, then you were probably good in science and didn't have Mr. Kay as a teacher for chemistry. He liked to yell, you see. Basically, heavy water is heavier than water because it has more particles in it. But let's get back to the observatory. The observatory was built so far underground to shield it from cosmic rays, which can interfere with experiments. I guess Sudbury's not just about big nickels anymore!

Places with Weird Marks You Can't Miss

People have left their Xs, signatures, graffiti and other marks announcing "I was here" in caves, on rocks and walls and on each other since time immemorial.

What follows is a sampling of how they've marked up Ontario.

OLD WALT
BON ECHO PROVINCIAL PARK

Old and new forms of graffiti mix at Bon Echo Provincial Park, just north of Belleville. A 1.5-kilometre-long sheer rock face rises 100 metres over Mazinaw Lake. The rock is known as "Old Walt," thanks to a turn-of-the-century suffragette named Flora MacDonald Denison, who is not to be mixed up with either the Flora MacDonald who helped Bonnie Prince Charlie nor the one that served as a cabinet minister in Brian Mulroney's government. The last Flora MacDonald may be getting a bit long in the tooth but certainly is not as old or as dead as the other two.

Flora MacDonald Dennison set up an eco-friendly retreat dedicated to the ideals of Walt Whitman on the Bon Echo site in 1910. She later owned and ran the nearby Bon Echo Inn. In 1919, she had Old Walt (the rock) dedicated to (or defaced, depending on your beliefs) Walt Whitman. A year later, she had some of Whitman's poetry inscribed in 30-centimetre-high lettering in the granite. The dedication actually reads:

Old Walt
1819–1919
Dedicated to the democratic ideals of
Walt Whitman
by
Horace Traubel and Flora MacDonald
"My foothold is tenon'd and mortised in granite
I laugh at what you call dissolution
And I know the amplitude of time."

The Horace Traubel mentioned in the rock inscription was a friend of Walt Whitman who claimed to see Whitman's ghost there near the dedicated/defaced rock. He later got carried away with all the Whitman ghost sightings and died on-site.

Before the really big Whitman words were added to the Old Walt rock, the ancient Algonkians had painted 260 images in ochre on the rock at water level. Called pictographs, they can still be seen today, which just goes to show that graffiti has been a valid human art form for a very long time!

PETROGLYPHS PROVINCIAL PARK
NORTH OF PETERBOROUGH

Canada's largest concentration of aboriginal rock carvings lies north of Peterborough in Petroglyphs Provincial Park. The 900 petroglyphs were probably carved by the Ojibwa people between 500 and 1000 years ago. The symbolic shapes spread out across a 60-metre by 35-metre almost flat stone surface. The petroglyph images include turtles, snakes, humans and a whole host of other wild creatures and objects. The site remains sacred to the Ojibwa who call it Kinomagewapkong—"The Rocks that Teach."

Agawa Bay lies 90 kilometres northwest of Sault Ste. Marie and within Lake Superior Provincial Park. The area is sacred to the Ojibwa people, and to show their respect for it, ancient Ojibwa left their marks on the sheer rock face known as Inscription Rock. Numerous red ochre and grease pictographs date back more than 200 years.

BIG GARGANTUAN & RIDICULOUSLY OVERSIZED

PATH

The world's largest underground shopping complex is Toronto's PATH. PATH is also known to most people who work in downtown Toronto as a winding way to get from Union Station to the Eaton Centre and slightly beyond without going outside. It's 27 kilometres of walkway that snakes its way between six major hotels such as the Royal York and Sheraton Centre, 50 office buildings such as First Canadian Place and Commerce Court, and connects attractions such as the CN Tower, Hockey Hall of Fame and Air Canada Centre. The building that is farthest north on the PATH network is the Bay and Dundas Street Bus Terminal. The southernmost point is the Toronto Convention Centre's south building. There are also more than 1200 stores and restaurants along the way, so if you get lost, there are more than a few places to sit and ponder your way out. PATH is not an acronym for anything except, well, it's a path—like an old First Nation's travelling path. Each letter in the PATH logo is, however, a different colour and represents a different direction. The P is red and points people south; the A is orange and points people to the west; the blue T helps them meander north; and the yellow H puts people squarely in an easterly direction. Makes sense, right? About as much as that colour-coded Terrorist Alert system that the Americans use. Coincidentally, both systems were developed by government organizations. Shocker, huh?

GLADSTONE HOTEL
TORONTO

The oldest continually operating hotel in Toronto is Parkdale's Gladstone Hotel. Built in 1889, the hotel had seen better days and had become just a seedy drinking establishment and a sort of flophouse until the new owners, the Zeidler family, had the hotel renovated in 2005. They commissioned local artists to leave their mark on 35 of the 51 rooms. Each of the artists was allowed to decorate in their own style. The result? The Roman Suite featuring "Orgy and Vomit" rooms, the Mike Harris Starvation Block and Farley Mowat's "Lost in the Barrens" room with real caribou! Not really. The real rooms include the bold and brash Biker Room, which is all red and black; the Teen Queen Room, which looks like a teenage girl's bedroom; and the Faux Naturelle Room, which is a woodsy retreat à la lesbian separatist commune meets storybook gardens.

FLATIRON BUILDING
TORONTO

Toronto's wedge-shaped Flatiron Building would be mark enough just because of its wedge shape. However, the red brick building, which was built in 1892 and is officially called the Gooderham Building, is famous for more than its age and architecturally unique shape. On the wide edge of the wedge, facing the Financial District, is a mural created by Derek Basant. The mural uses a *tromp l'oeil* effect to make the building look as though it's made of canvas and is fluttering in the wind where its edges aren't tacked down. The mural is called "Tromp d'Oeil" and the building is wedged between Front and Wellington Streets at Church Street.

BIG
GARGANTUAN &
RIDICULOUSLY
OVERSIZED

Jumbo

In St. Thomas, there is a life-sized statue of Jumbo, P.T. Barnum's famous giant elephant. The citizens of St. Thomas erected the statue in 1985 to commemorate the 100th anniversary of Jumbo's death. Why commemorate the death of an elephant? The demise of the unfortunate pachyderm was the result of a run-in with a train in St. Thomas. Or as a military spokesperson might say, Jumbo became collateral damage.

The Weirdest
of the Weird

In this chapter I finally get to show my true colours and reveal how I really feel about all the weird places in Ontario.

Here are my nominations for Ontario's "Weirdest of the Weird."

WEIRDEST LARGE ATTRACTION

Noah's Ark replete with Pizza Hut at Logos Land in Cobden. Not even Cecil B. DeMille would do this to the Old Testament.

WEIRDEST UFO-RELATED PLACE

The "World's First UFO Sighting Station" at Shirley's Bay because, let's face it, though Shirley's Bay was the first official UFO sighting station, we all know there are a lot more unofficial ones hovering about.

WEIRDEST FORMER WEIRD SITE

Autohenge in Oshawa, because its creator, Bill Lishman, is a true original and because it sounds like a lot more fun than the original I saw on the Salisbury Plain in England.

WEIRDEST MONSTER-VIEWING LOCATION

Cobalt, because a blond-haired Bigfoot named Old Yellow Top trumps a sea monster any day.

WEIRDEST NATURALLY OCCURRING PLACE

A toss up between:

Fathom Five National Marine Park, which has a cool name and weird ancient and underwater stuff, and the Ouimet Canyon, which has a great creation story.

BIG
GARGANTUAN &
RIDICULOUSLY
OVERSIZED

Mosquito

In the town of Upsala, northwest of Thunder Bay, there is a kitschy statue at the Can-Op service station of a giant mosquito carrying off a man. The mosquito is double the size of the 2-metre-tall man it is carrying. It also has a knife and fork in its hands...legs...feet...or whatever those appendages are called, and it's been there since 1997. I guess a man-size meal takes a long time for a giant mosquito to eat! Actually, the monument is not a replica of something real—it's just there to remind people that mosquitoes in these here parts are quite enormous. No kidding! Just imagine the bite mark it would leave!

WEIRDEST STREET OF DISTRACTION

Church Street in Toronto, because no matter what, heads are always turning!

WEIRDEST PLACE TO CELEBRATE

Wiarton, because albino woodchucks rule!

WEIRDEST NON-THREATENING GHOSTLY PLACE

Mackenzie House in Toronto, because the toilet-flushing W.L. Mackenzie sounds like a lot of rabble-rousing fun. Also, because the staff at MacKenzie House are into it.

WEIRDEST FRESH-AIR FREAK LOCALE

Stratford with its Headless Horseman, because he probably doesn't even know he's outside.

WEIRDEST GRUESOME OR GHOULISH PLACE

The Ottawa youth hostel, because it scares the heck out of me and I'm never in a million years going to go there!

WEIRDEST FOOLISH PLACE

Clifton Hill in Niagara Falls, because at the attractions on this street, they'd just as soon separate you from your money as scare you!

WEIRDEST "YOU'VE GOT TO BE KIDDING" PLACE

Sudbury's Solar Neutrino Observatory, because it's way out there even though it's way down there.

WEIRDEST RECORD-BREAKING PLACE

Yonge Street, because it's weird all the way from Lake Ontario in Toronto to the Minnesota border...and because outsiders are jealous of its record-breaking length.

WEIRDEST PLACE WHERE MARKS WERE LEFT BEHIND

Old Walt in Bon Echo Provincial Park, because it combines graffiti, archaeology, feminism, ecology and literature. Now that's weird!

And, finally, the hands down, nothing comes close to it, no holds barred...

WEIRDEST OF ONTARIO'S WEIRD PLACES: NIAGARA FALLS!

Niagara Falls is currently and probably always will be the weirdest place in all of Ontario. It's got amazing natural beauty, wonder and power with the Horseshoe Falls; it's got the most amazing set of wet attractions with the Journey Behind the Falls and the Maid of the Mist; it's got death-defying reality with all the people who try to go over the falls in a barrel; it's got visiting UFOs that hover and possibly aliens running the power plants; it's got tacky tourist stuff with Clifton Hill and the Haunted House, Castle Drakula, the House of Frankenstein, the Criminals Hall of Fame, Alien Encounter, Dinosaur Park Miniature Golf, the Fun House, the Great Canadian Midway, Guinness World of Records Museum and so much more. Combine all that with two casinos, heart-shaped beds and honeymooners, and you've got one gigantic piece of weird!

REDUCE, REUSE, RECYCLE

These are the three Rs of the environmental movement. They can also be applied to this book, now that you've reached the end. Provided that you aren't one of those people that start at the end.

The point of this little book, the underlying premise, is this:

Reduce your dependency on the Internet, television and Pony Express dispatches—read a book instead.

Reuse this fine piece of literature after you're done with it. Whether you loved it or just liked it, don't throw it away. Reuse it to its fullest. It could be placed inside a beautifully hand-crafted and homemade display case with other writings by your favourite authors. Or each of the 168 pages could be reused as witty napkins at your next cocktail party. Or, if worse comes to worse and you're pinched for cash, you could use the whole book as kindling or perhaps the individual pages as toilet paper. A little rough, I know, but hey, no pain, no gain! The toilet paper suggestion is not my own idea. I took it from the standard issue Big Blue Machine, Tory Party platform book under the heading of "100 Helpful Hints to Have an Assistant Yell at the Poor People in Your Riding on Welfare Bums Appreciation Day."

Recycle this book. Well, I don't want to hit this one too heavily, but the great thing about a book is that you can share it with others. What? Say it ain't so! No, my friends, it is so. This book will not self-destruct after you've finished with it. Always remember, though, in publishing, margins are low, deadlines are tight and we need to sell a lot of books to stay solvent. So if you do recycle *Weird Ontario Places,* realize that every time you do, a writer somewhere is going to go without ink. And what is a writer without ink? Just a lowly thinker. And we all know where thinking leads. Anarchy, Utopia or somewhere in between, which I believe is an all-expenses-paid stay for weeks, months or years at the U.S. prison at Guantanamo Bay.

Alas, all good things must come to an end—half-baked good things as well as full-baked and burned ones. And so it is with mixed emotions (or perhaps cramps from sitting at this desk for so many weeks) that I bid a fond farewell to *Weird Ontario Places*, and I think, the *Weird Places* series of books as a whole. There are or will be other editions of the various weird regions of Canada—*Weird Alberta Places, Weird Maritimes Places, Super Weird and Unnatural British Columbia Places*. Other authors will write those highly entertaining guides. I hope they have as much fun researching and writing those books as I know that all of you have had reading them. Or not?

The most disappointing thing about writing this book, as with previously writing *Weird Canadian Places*, is that I had to omit hundreds, or maybe thousands, of places that I find weird. But hey, they weren't weird enough and didn't make the cut. There is only so much room and there are only so many suitably large and very slow-growing paper-producing trees. So, if some weird place that is close to your heart didn't make the cut, blame the trees!

If you've got suggestions, nominations for the next round of weird places or comments about what you've read, we'd love to hear from you, so write to us at bluebikebooks@yahoo.ca.

And so my friends, I leave you with this: Go forth and seek out the strange, embrace all that is weird and find out what really puts the "Oh!" in Ontario.

ABOUT THE AUTHOR

Dan de Figueiredo

Dan de Figueiredo has been a journalist, television writer, film-maker and playwright. His love for words began when his aunt and uncle gave him a copy of *Robinson Crusoe*, and he has never looked back. After earning his BA in political science at McMaster, followed by a BAA in journalism from Ryerson, Dan worked on the Canadian edition of *Who Wants to Be a Millionaire*, *Reach for the Top*, numerous television and theatre productions and several independent films. He is currently a freelance television writer, producer and researcher.

ABOUT THE ILLUSTRATORS

Graham Johnson

Graham Johnson is an Edmonton-based illustrator and graphic designer. When he isn't drawing or designing, he...well...he's always drawing or designing! On the off-chance you catch him not doing one of those things, he's probably cooking, playing tennis or poring over other illustrations.

Roger Garcia

Roger Garcia immigrated to Canada from El Salvador at the age of seven. Because of the language barrier, he had to find a way to communicate with other kids. That's when he discovered the art of tracing. It wasn't long before he mastered this highly skilled technique, and by age 14, he was drawing weekly cartoons for the *Edmonton Examiner*. He taught himself to paint and sculpt; then in high school and college, Roger skipped class to hide in the art room all day in order to further explore his talent. Currently, Roger's work can be seen in a local weekly newspaper and in places around Edmonton.